table
toppers

Celebrating the Great Outdoors

Landauer Books

table toppers

Celebrating the Great Outdoors

by Debbie Field
for Granola Girl® Designs

This book was designed, produced, and published by Landauer Books
A division of Landauer Corporation
3100 101st Street, Ste. A, Urbandale, Iowa 50322
www.landauercorp.com   800/557-2144

President/Publisher: Jeramy Lanigan Landauer
Vice President of Sales & Operations: Kitty Jacobson
Managing Editor: Jeri Simon
Art Director: Laurel Albright
Project Editor: Rhonda Matus
Photographer: Craig Anderson

ISBN 13: 978-0-9793711-5-8
ISBN 10: 0-9793711-5-5

This book is printed on acid-free paper.
Printed in China

10 9 8 7 6 5 4 3 2

Table Toppers by Granola Girl® Designs
Library of Congress Control Number: 2008920304

introduction

Celebrate every season with a touch of nature. With the projects in this book you'll discover how easy it is to bring the outdoors to your table.

Debbie Field for Granola Girl® Designs has created 16 original table topper projects to celebrate the seasons of the year. Each quick-to-complete, quilted, nature-driven table accent has clear, step-by-step instructions and full-size appliqué patterns.

Projects range from a radiant iris table runner with complementary place mats for spring to a seasonal silent night table topper for winter. Once you begin, you'll find it difficult to stop until every surface in your home celebrates the season.

Debbie Field

A special thank you to my creative team for your individual talents.

Delores Farmer
Sue Carter
Sue Longeville
Cindy Kujawa

Contents

8

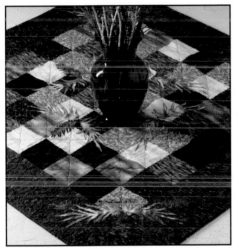

general instructions

Assemble the tools and supplies to complete the project. In addition to basic cutting and sewing tools, the following will make cutting and sewing easier: small sharp scissors to cut appliqué shapes, rotary cutter and mat, extra rotary blades, and a transparent ruler with markings.

Replace the sewing machine needle each time you start a project to maintain even stitches and to prevent skipped stitches and broken needles during the project. Clean the machine after every project to remove lint and to keep it running smoothly.

The projects shown are made with unwashed fabrics. If you prewash fabrics, purchase extra yardage to allow for shrinkage. The 100-percent cottons and flannels used in the wilderness quilts and accessories are from Debbie's Granola Girl® collections: Marblecake Basics, Boundary Waters, Deer Camp, and Wood, Water and Wildlife fabric lines manufactured by Troy Corporation. Ask for them by name at your local quilt shop.

Please read through the project instructions before cutting and sewing. Square the fabric before cutting by placing the folded fabric on your cutting mat. Align one of the horizontal lines on the ruler with the folded edge nearest you. Place your rotary cutter at the right edge of your ruler and cut fabric from selvage to selvage. Square your fabric again after cutting 3 or 4 strips.

To create accurate half-square triangles, align your ruler diagonally from corner to corner on each fabric square and cut.

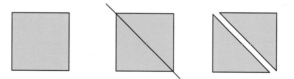

Sew with 1/4" seam allowances throughout, unless stated otherwise in the instructions, and check seam allowance accuracy to prevent compounding even slight errors. Press seams toward the darker fabric when possible. When pressing small joined pieces, press in the direction that creates less bulk.

basic appliqué

Please note that the printed appliqué templates are reversed. Trace and cut the templates as printed, unless the illustrations and photos indicate to reverse the templates. For appliqués that face the opposite direction, trace and reverse the template. Dashed lines indicate design overlap.

Trace the appliqué template to the fusible webbing with a fine tip marker or sharp pencil, allowing space to cut 1/4" beyond the traced lines. Position the fusible web on the wrong side of the appliqué fabric. Follow the manufacturer's instructions to fuse the webbing to the fabric. Allow the fabric to cool and cut along the traced line. Remove the paper backing and follow the pattern placement to position the appliqué pieces on the background fabrics.

Use lightweight tear-away stabilizer to machine appliqué. Place the stabilizer beneath the fabric layers and use a small, zigzag stitch to sew around each shape, smoothly covering the raw fabric edge. The stitch is meant to secure the outermost edge of an appliqué shape in place. Your stitches should lie close together without appearing bunched up. If your machine has stitch options, use them to detail appliqués. After the stitching is complete, remove the stabilizer according to the manufacturer's instructions.

Trace

Position and Fuse

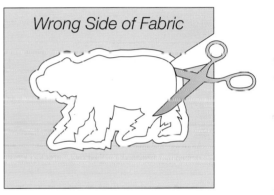

Cut

Peel   *Arrange and Fuse*

basic binding

1. Cut the binding strips for your project from selvage to selvage. Join them for a continuous length by sewing the short ends of the binding strips, right sides together, with diagonal seams. Trim 1/4" from the sewn line and press open, as shown. Fold the strip in half lengthwise, wrong sides together, and press.

2. Match the raw edges of the folded strip to the quilt top, along a lower edge and approximately 6" from a corner, allowing approximately 6" free to join to the opposite end of the binding. Avoid placing binding seams on corners. Sew the binding to the quilt top with a 1/4" seam allowance.

3. At the first corner, stop 1/4" from the corner, backstitch, raise the presser foot and needle, and rotate the quilt 90 degrees. Fold the binding back onto itself to create a miter.

4. Fold it along the adjacent seam, matching raw edges. Continue sewing to the next corner and repeat the mitered corner process.

5. Where the binding ends meet, fold under one binding edge 1/4", encase the opposite binding edge, and stitch it to the quilt top.

6. Trim the batting and backing fabric even with the quilt top and binding. Fold the binding strip to the back of the quilt and handsew it in place with a blind stitch. Sign and date the quilt, including the recipient's name if it is a gift.

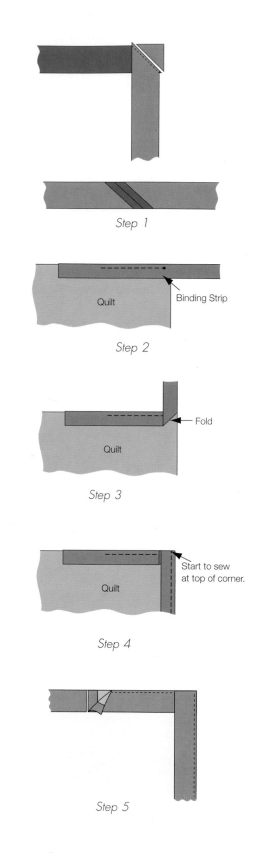

Step 1

Step 2

Step 3

Step 4

Step 5

basic quilting

- **Individual Motifs** Any design that stands alone, such as a flower or leaf, is a great choice for quilting the plain blocks in an alternating block quilt. You can often use a portion of an isolated motif to fill spaces in patchwork patterns. Designs along a border can also be repeated. Individual motifs can be square, circular, or oval—the range of possibilities is vast.

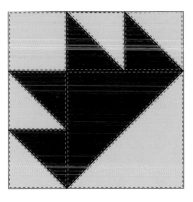

- **Stitching-in-the-Ditch** is stitching very close to the seams in a block. Patchwork blocks generally involve a lot of seam allowances. To avoid having to stitch through more layers than necessary with this type of block, try stitching in the ditch along the side of the seam with the least amount of bulk.

- **Outline Quilting** is a series of 1/4" stitching lines that outline the shape of the design in your block. You can choose to use this stitch to fill in the entire background section of your block.

- **Meander or Stipple Quilting** has an overall pattern that resembles the curvy pieces of a jigsaw puzzle. Ideally the quilting lines don't touch or overlap one another. It is a nice choice for covering large areas quickly or adding texture behind an appliqué shape to make it stand out.

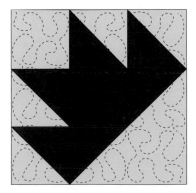

table runner
radiant iris

Materials

Finished size is approximately
21" x 40-1/2"

*Refer to the general instructions on
pages 6–7 before starting this project.*

3/8 yard of light yellow fabric
for center

1/4 yard of green fabric
for inner border

1/2 yard flower-motif fabric
for outer border

1/2 yard of dark green fabric for
corner squares and binding

Fabric scraps of dark green (stems,
leaves), blue (petals), and
dark yellow (flower center)

1–1/3 yards of backing fabric

27" x 47" piece of batting

Lightweight paper-backed
fusible web

Lightweight tear-away stabilizer

Sulky® thread to match appliqués

*Note: Fabrics are based on
44"-wide fabrics that have not been
washed. Please purchase accordingly.*

instructions

Cutting

From light yellow fabric:
Cut 1 rectangle — 11" x 30-1/2" for center.

From green fabric:
Cut 3 strips — 1-1/2" x 44",
from the strips cut 2 — 1-1/2" x 30-1/2"
inner border strips
and 2 — 1-1/2" x 13" inner border strips.

From flower-motif fabric:
Cut 3 strips — 4-1/2" x 44",
from the strips cut 2 — 4-1/2" x 32-1/2"
outer border strips
and 2 — 4-1/2" x 13" outer border strips.

From dark green fabric:
Cut 1 strip — 4-1/2" x 44",
from the strip cut 4 — 4-1/2" corner squares.
Cut 4 strips — 3" x 44" for binding.

From backing fabric:
Cut 1 — 27" x 47" rectangle.

Assembling the Table Runner

1. Sew the 1–1/2" x 30–1/2" green inner border strips to the long edges of the 11" x 30–1/2" light yellow center rectangle as shown. Press the seam allowances toward the border.

2. Sew the 1–1/2" x 13" green inner border strips to the short edges of the center rectangle as shown. Press the seam allowances toward the border.

3. Sew the 4–1/2" x 32–1/2" flower-motif outer border strips to the long edges of the inner border as shown. Press the seam allowances toward the outer border.

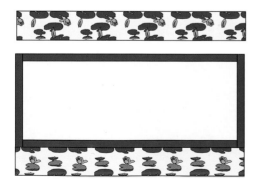

4. Sew a 4–1/2" dark green corner square to each short edge of the two 4–1/2" x 13" flower-motif outer border strips as shown. Press the seam allowances toward the squares.

5. Sew the pieced outer border from Step 4 to the short edges of the inner border as shown. Press the seam allowances toward the outer border.

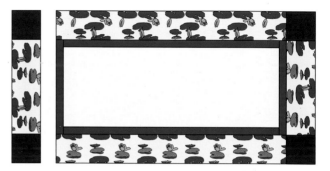

Adding the Appliqués

1. Using the appliqué templates on pages 17 and 18, trace the shapes onto the paper side of the fusible web and cut out as desired.

2. Referring to Basic Appliqué instructions on pages 10 and 11, prepare the fabric appliqué pieces, position and fuse them on the center rectangle, and machine appliqué with matching thread and stabilizer.

Finishing the Table Runner

Layer the backing fabric, batting and appliquéd top. Baste the layers together. Hand- or machine-quilt as desired. Finish the table runner by sewing binding to the edges, following the steps in Basic Binding on page 12.

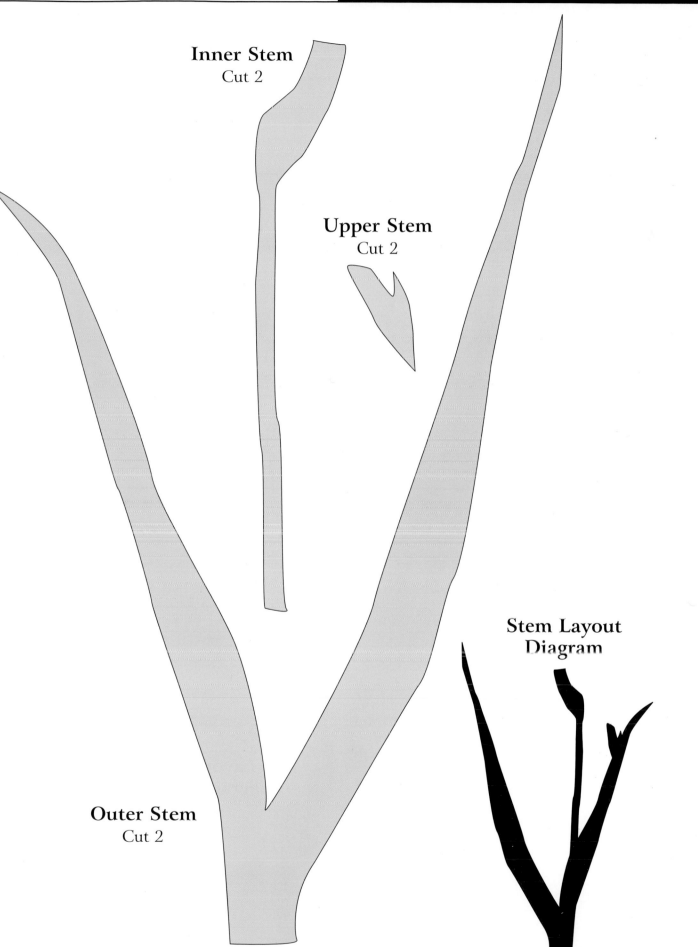

Inner Stem
Cut 2

Upper Stem
Cut 2

**Stem Layout
Diagram**

Outer Stem
Cut 2

17

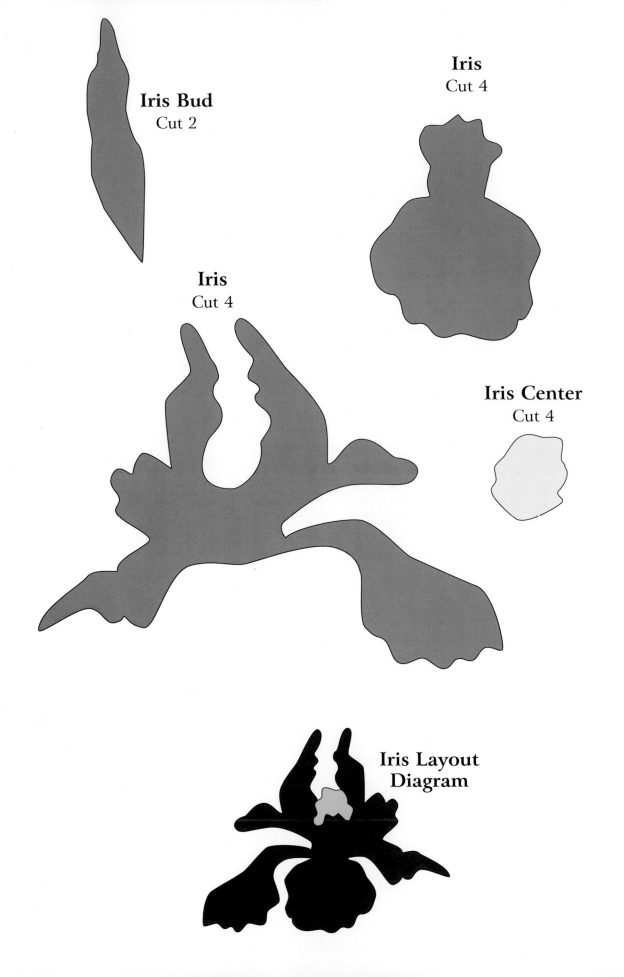

Iris Bud
Cut 2

Iris
Cut 4

Iris
Cut 4

Iris Center
Cut 4

Iris Layout Diagram

Radiant Iris Table Runner

place mats
woodland floral

instructions

Materials

Finished size is approximately
14–1/2" x 19–1/2"

Materials list is for 4 place mats.

Refer to the general instructions on pages 6–7 before starting this project.

3/4 yard of navy flower-motif fabric for right front

3/8 yard of light yellow fabric for left front

1 yard of dark green fabric for sashing, border, and binding

Fabric scraps of dark yellow (flower petals and centers), rust (flower centers), two dark greens (stems, leaves, flower centers), and two light greens (stems, leaves)

1–1/2 yards of backing fabric

Four 20" x 25" pieces of batting

Lightweight paper-backed fusible web

Lightweight tear-away stabilizer

Sulky® threads to match appliqués

Note: Fabrics are based on 44"-wide fabrics that have not been washed. Please purchase accordingly.

Cutting

From navy flower-motif fabric:
    Cut 2 strips — 12–1/2" x 44",
        from the strips cut 4 — 12–1/2" right front squares.

From light yellow fabric:
    Cut 2 strips — 4–1/2" x 44",
        from the strips cut 4 — 4–1/2" x 12–1/2" left front rectangles.

From dark green fabric:
    Cut 8 strips — 1 1/2" x 44",
        from the strips cut 4 — 1–1/2" x 12–1/2" sashing strips
        and 8 — 1–1/2" x 17–1/2" border strips
        and 8 — 1–1/2" x 14–1/2" border strips.
    Cut 7 strips — 2–3/4" x 44" for binding

From backing fabric:
    Cut 4 — 20" x 25" rectangles.

Assembling the Place Mat Top

1. Sew together a 4–1/2" x 12–1/2" light yellow left front rectangle, a 1–1/2" x 12–1/2" dark green sashing strip, and a 12–1/2" navy flower-motif right front square as shown. Press the seam allowances toward the sashing.

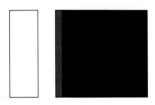

2. Sew a 1–1/2" x 17–1/2" dark green border strip to the top and bottom edges of the place mat as shown. Press the seam allowances toward the border.

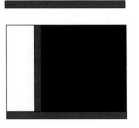

3. Sew a 1–1/2" x 14–1/2" dark green border strip to the left and right edges of the place mat as shown. Press the seam allowances toward the border.

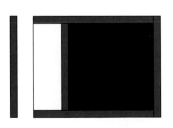

4. Repeat Steps 1 to 3 for each place mat.

Adding the Appliqués

1. Using the appliqué templates on pages 23 and 24, trace the shapes onto the paper side of the fusible web and cut out as desired.

2. Referring to Basic Appliqué instructions on pages 10 and 11, prepare the fabric appliqué pieces, position and fuse them on the light yellow rectangle, and machine appliqué with matching thread and stabilizer.

Finishing the Place Mats

Layer the backing rectangle, batting and appliquéd top for each place mat. Baste the layers together. Hand- or machine-quilt as desired. Finish the place mats by sewing binding to the edges, following the steps in Basic Binding on page 12.

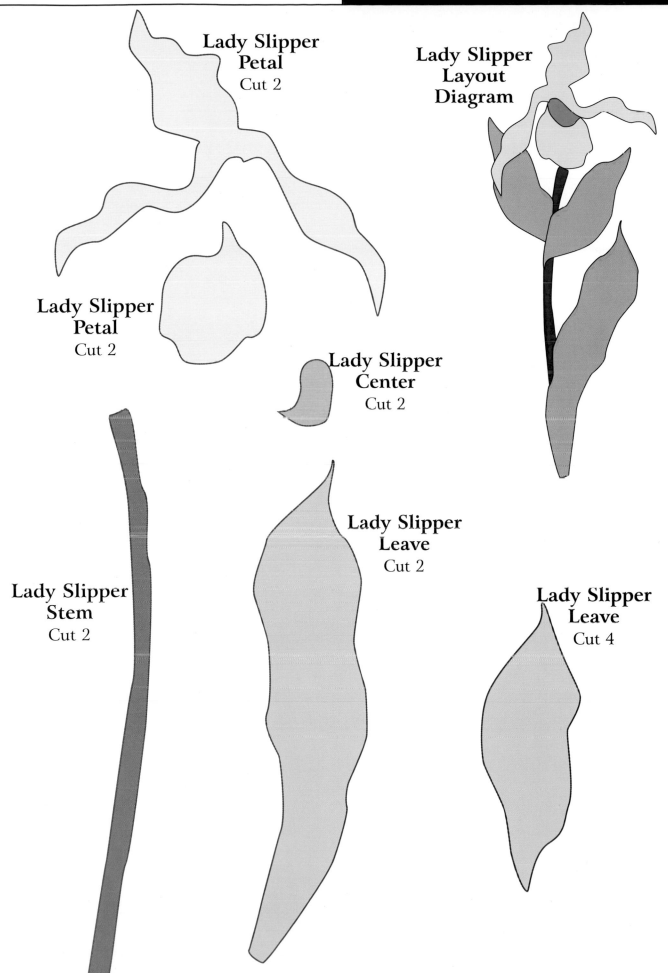

Lady Slipper Petal
Cut 2

Lady Slipper Layout Diagram

Lady Slipper Petal
Cut 2

Lady Slipper Center
Cut 2

Lady Slipper Stem
Cut 2

Lady Slipper Leave
Cut 2

Lady Slipper Leave
Cut 4

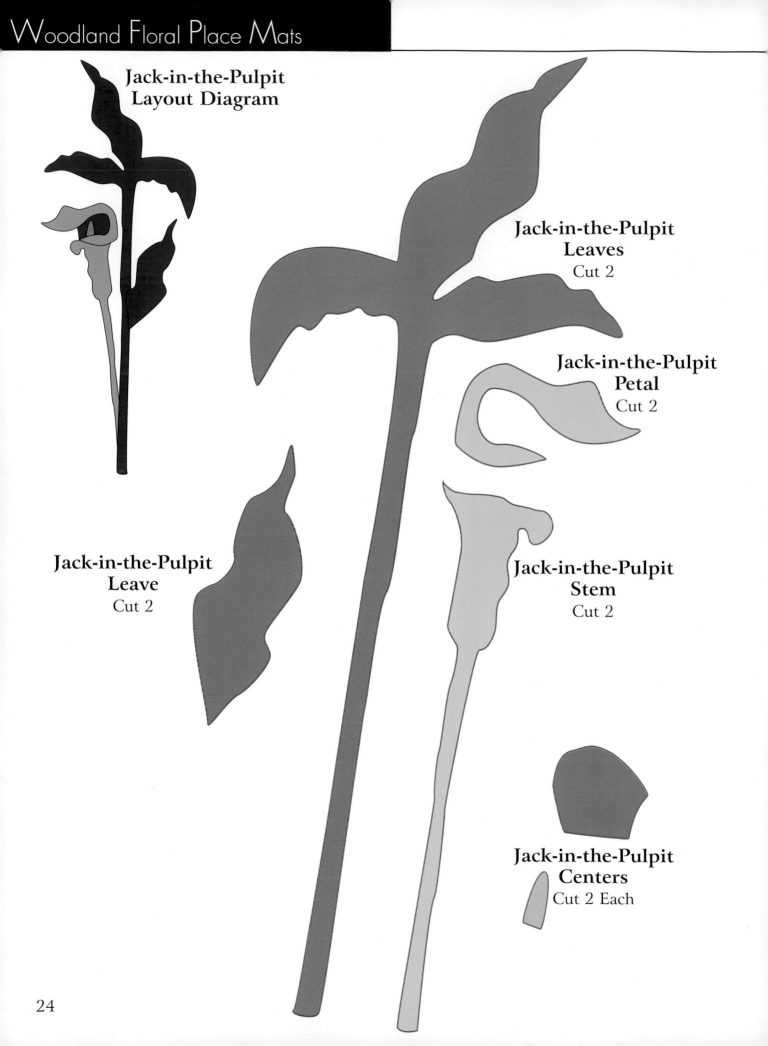

Woodland Floral Place Mats

Jack-in-the-Pulpit Layout Diagram

Jack-in-the-Pulpit Leaves
Cut 2

Jack-in-the-Pulpit Petal
Cut 2

Jack-in-the-Pulpit Leave
Cut 2

Jack-in-the-Pulpit Stem
Cut 2

Jack-in-the-Pulpit Centers
Cut 2 Each

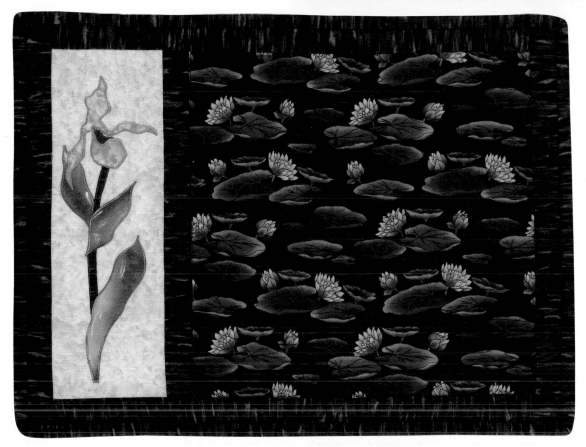

Lady Slipper Place Mat

Jack-in-the-Pulpit Place Mat

table topper
bear paw picnic

Materials

Finished size is approximately
45–1/2" x 45–1/2"

*Refer to the general instructions on
pages 6–7 before starting this project.*

3/4 yard of blue fabric
for blocks

1–1/4 yards of light green fabric
for blocks and binding

1/4 yard of dark green fabric
for sashing

1/6 yard of tan fabric
for sashing

1–1/8 yards of navy fabric
for border and cornerstone square

3 yards of backing fabric

52" square of batting

*Note: Fabrics are based on 44"-wide
fabrics that have not been washed.
Please purchase accordingly.*

Cutting

From blue fabric:
  Cut 1 strip — 10–7/8" x 44",
      from strip cut 2 — 10–7/8" squares.
      Cut squares in half diagonally to make 4 half-square triangles.
  Cut 2 strips — 5–7/8" x 44",
      from strips cut 8 — 5–7/8" squares.
      Cut squares in half diagonally to make 16 half-square triangles.

From light green fabric:
  Cut 1 strip — 10–7/8" x 44",
      from strip cut 2 — 10–7/8" squares.
      Cut squares in half diagonally to make 4 half-square triangles.
  Cut 2 strips — 5–7/8" x 44",
      from strips cut 8 — 5–7/8" squares.
      Cut squares in half diagonally to make 16 half-square triangles.
  Cut 1 strip — 5–1/2" x 44",
      from strip cut 4 — 5–1/2" squares.
  Cut 5 strips   2 1/2" x 44" for binding.

From dark green fabric:
  Cut 2 strips — 3–1/2" x 44",
      from strips cut 4 — 3–1/2" x 10–1/2" sashing strips.

From tan fabric:
  Cut 1 strip — 3–1/2" x 44",
      from strip cut 4 — 3–1/2" x 5–1/2" sashing strips.

From navy fabric:
  Cut 5 strips — 6–1/2" x 44" for border.
  Cut 1 — 3–1/2" square.

From backing fabric:
  Cut 2 rectangles — 27" x 52".

Assembly

1. Sew together a small blue half-square triangle and a small light green half-square triangle as shown. Press the seam allowances toward the dark triangle. Repeat to make 16 Unit A. Press the seam allowances toward the dark triangles.

Make 16 Unit A

2. Sew together 8 Unit A in pairs as shown to make 4 Unit B. Press the seam allowances toward the dark fabric.

Make 4 Unit B

3. Sew the remaining 8 Unit A together in pairs as shown to make 4 Unit C. Press the seam allowances toward the dark fabric.

Make 4 Unit C

4. Sew a 5–1/2″ light green square to each Unit C as shown to make 4 Unit D. Press the seam allowances toward the square.

Make 4 Unit D

5. Sew together the large blue and light green half-square triangles as shown to make 4 Unit E. Press the seam allowances toward the dark triangles.

Make 4 Unit E

6. Sew a Unit B to each Unit E as shown to make 4 Unit F. Press the seam allowances toward the large blue triangle.

Make 4 Unit F

7. Sew a Unit D to each Unit F as shown to make 4 Unit G blocks. Press the seam allowances toward Unit F.

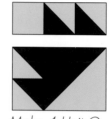

Make 4 Unit G

Assembling the Table Topper

1. Sew a 3–1/2″ x 10–1/2″ dark green sashing strip to each 3–1/2″ x 5–1/2″ tan sashing strip as shown to make 4 Unit H. Press the seam allowances toward the dark fabric.

Make 4 Unit H

2. Sew together 2 Unit G blocks with 1 Unit H as shown to make 1 Unit I. Press the seam allowances toward the sashing. Repeat to make 2 Unit I.

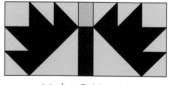

Make 2 Unit I

3. Sew together 2 Unit H with the 3–1/2″ navy cornerstone square as shown to form 1 Unit J. Press the seam allowances toward the sashing.

Make 1 Unit J

4. Sew together 2 Unit I with Unit J as shown to complete the table topper center. Press the seam allowances toward the sashing.

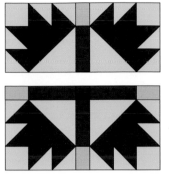

5. Measure the width of the table topper through the center for the top and bottom border measurement. Use this measurement to cut 2 lengths from the 6–1/2"-wide navy border strips. Sew the lengths to the top and bottom edges of the table topper center. Press seams toward the border.

6. Sew together the remaining 6–1/2"-wide navy border strips. Measure the length of the table topper through the center, including the top and bottom borders, for the side border measurement.

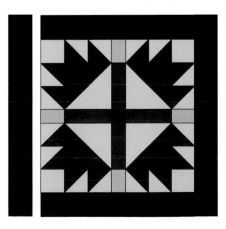

Use this measurement to cut 2 lengths from the 6–1/2" wide border strip. Sew the lengths to the left and right edges of the table topper center. Press seams toward the border.

Finishing the Table Topper

1. Sew together the 27" x 52" backing rectangles along one long edge, using a 1/2-inch seam allowance. Press the seam allowances open.

2. Layer the pieced backing, batting and table topper top. Baste the layers together. Hand- or machine-quilt as desired.

3. Sew binding to the edges of the table topper, following the steps in Basic Binding on page 12.

Bear Paw Picnic Table Topper

table runner
shore lunch

Materials

Finished size is approximately
23–1/2" x 47"

*Refer to the general instructions on
pages 6–7 before starting this project.*

1/2 yard of celery green fabric
for center

1/6 yard of blue fabric for water

1/3 yard of brown fabric
for sashing and inner border

7/8 yard of tree-motif fabric for outer
border and binding

8" x 16" piece of black woodgrain-
motif fabric for bears' body and feet

8" x 14" piece of dark
brown fabric for bears' head,
eyes, nose, and arms

10" x 11" piece of dark green
woodgrain-motif for trees

Fabric scraps of gold (feet, ears),
light brown (face), dark brown
(basket lid), light green (fish), and
light brown woodgrain-motif
(tree trunk, basket)

1–1/2 yards of backing fabric

30" x 53" piece of batting

Lightweight paper-backed
fusible web

Lightweight tear-away stabilizer

Sulky® thread to match appliqués

*Note: Fabrics are based on 44"-wide
fabrics that have not been washed.
Please purchase accordingly.*

instructions

Cutting

From celery green fabric:
    Cut 1 — 14–1/2" x 27" center rectangle.

From blue fabric:
    Cut 1 strip — 4–1/2" x 44",
        from the strip cut 2 — 4–1/2" x 14–1/2" rectangles.

From brown fabric:
    Cut 4 strips — 2" x 44",
        from the strips cut 2 — 2" x 14–1/2" sashing strips
        and 2 — 2" x 38" inner border strips
        and 2 — 2" x 17–1/2" inner border strips.

From tree-motif fabric:
    Cut 4 strips — 3–1/2" x 44",
        from the strips cut 2 — 3–1/2" x 41" outer border strips
        and 2 — 3–1/2" x 23–1/2" outer border strips.
    Cut 4 strips — 3" x 44" for binding.

From backing fabric:
    Cut 1 — 30" x 53" rectangle.

Assembling the Table Runner Top

1. Sew the 2" x 14–1/2" brown sashing strips to the short edges of the 14–1/2" x 27" celery green rectangle as shown. Press the seam allowances toward the sashing.

2. Sew a 4–1/2" x 14–1/2" blue rectangle to each sashing strip as shown. Press the seam allowances toward the sashing.

3. Sew the 2" x 38" brown inner border strips to the long edges of the table runner top as shown. Press the seam allowances toward the border.

4. Sew the 2" x 17–1/2" brown inner border strips to the short edges of the table runner top as shown. Press the seam allowances toward the border.

5. Sew the 3–1/2" x 41" tree-motif outer border strips to the long edges of the inner border. Press the seam allowances toward the outer border.

6. Sew the 3–1/2" x 23–1/2" tree-motif outer border strips to the short edges of the inner border. Press the seam allowances toward the outer border.

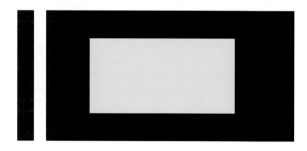

Adding the Appliqués

1. Using the appliqué templates on pages 33, 34, and 35, trace the shapes onto the paper side of the fusible web and cut out as directed.

2. Referring to Basic Appliqué instructions on pages 10 and 11, prepare the fabric appliqué pieces, position and fuse them on the table runner top, and machine appliqué with matching thread and stabilizer.

Finishing the Table Runner

Layer the backing fabric, batting and appliquéd top. Baste the layers together. Hand- or machine-quilt as desired. Finish the table runner by sewing binding to the edges, following the steps in Basic Binding on page 12.

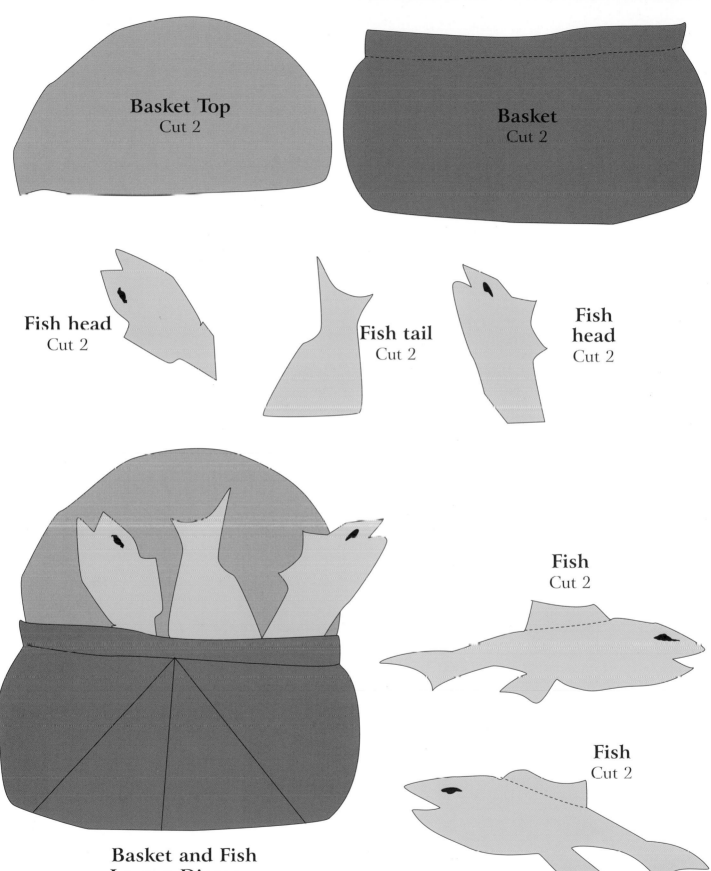

Basket Top
Cut 2

Basket
Cut 2

Fish head
Cut 2

Fish tail
Cut 2

Fish head
Cut 2

Fish
Cut 2

Fish
Cut 2

**Basket and Fish
Layout Diagram**

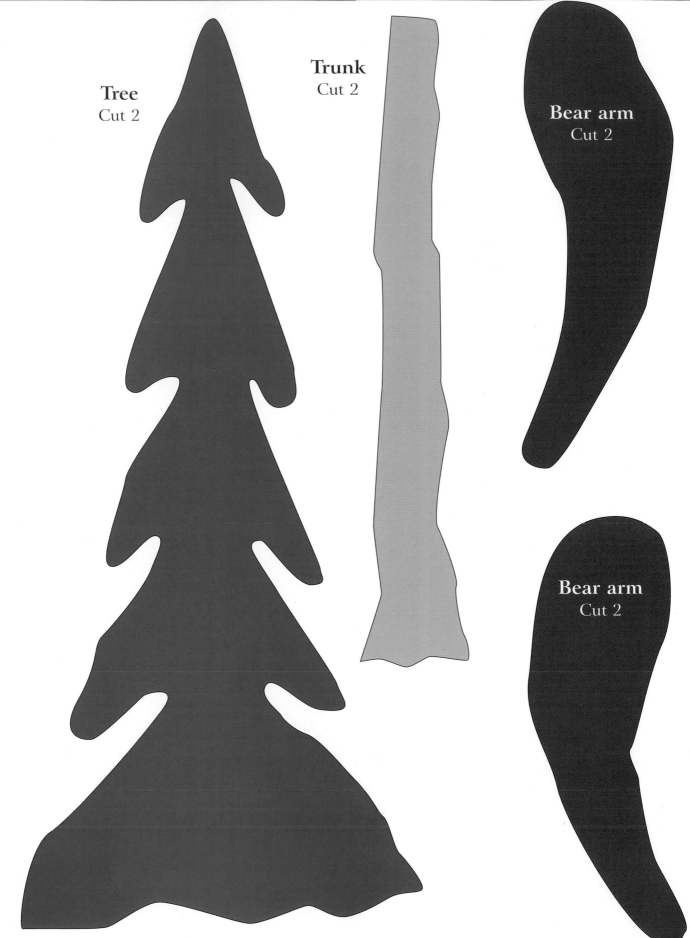

Tree
Cut 2

Trunk
Cut 2

Bear arm
Cut 2

Bear arm
Cut 2

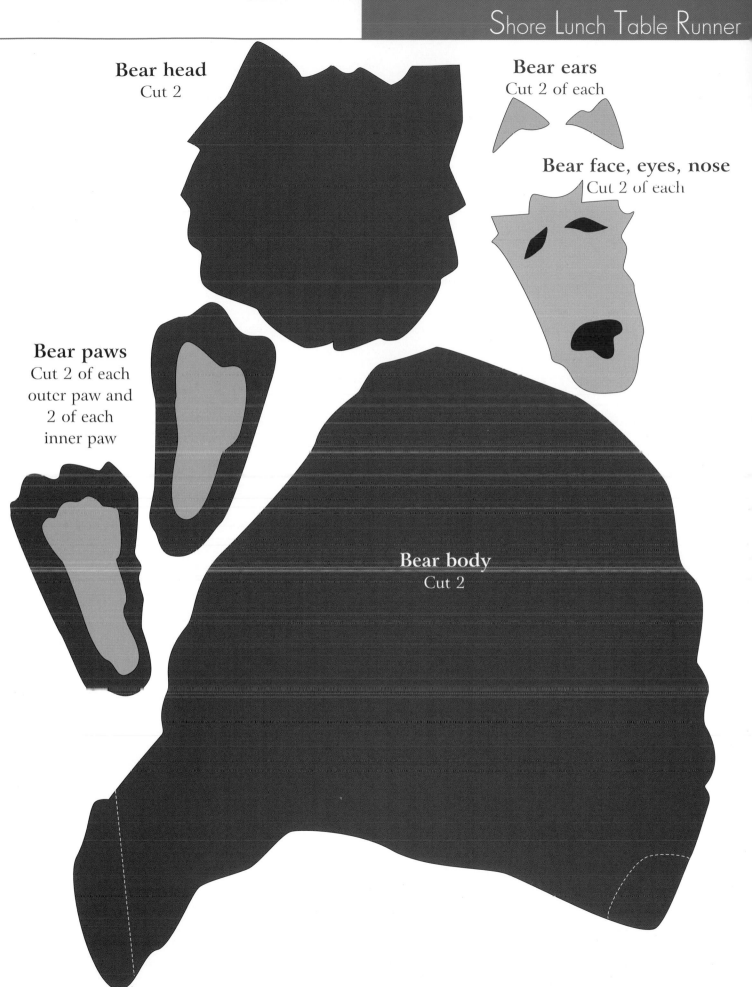

Bear head
Cut 2

Bear ears
Cut 2 of each

Bear face, eyes, nose
Cut 2 of each

Bear paws
Cut 2 of each
outer paw and
2 of each
inner paw

Bear body
Cut 2

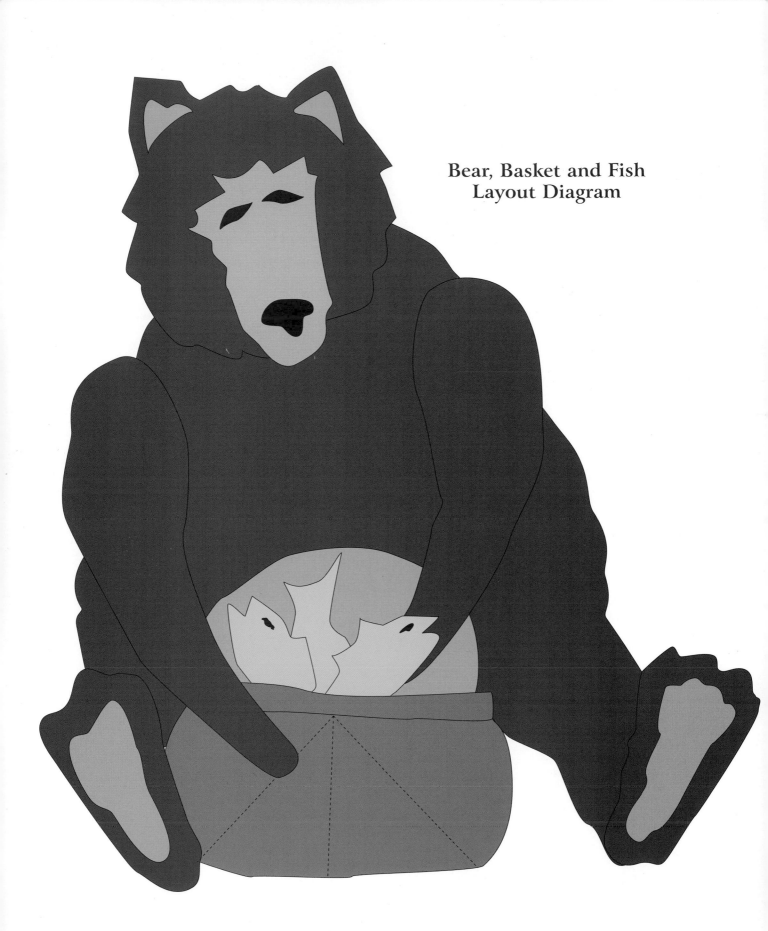

**Bear, Basket and Fish
Layout Diagram**

Shore Lunch Table Runner

table runner
loons on the shore

Materials

Finished size is approximately
28–1/2" x 17–1/2"

*Refer to the general instructions on
pages 6–7 before starting this project.*

1/2 yard of black fabric
for background

1 fat quarter of light blue fabric
for oval

5/8 yard of dark green fabric
for border and binding

Fabric scraps of dark brown
(ground), two blues (water, cloud),
white (loons), dark green (island),
black (loons), light green (trees), light
brown (trees, tongues), gold and
brown (rocks)

1/4 yard of dark brown fabric
for tongues

3/4 yard of backing fabric

24" x 35" piece of batting

Lightweight paper-backed
fusible web

Lightweight tear-away stabilizer

Sulky® thread to match appliqués

Black DMC Perle Cotton, Size 8

*Note: Fabrics are based on 44"-wide
fabrics that have not been washed.
Please purchase accordingly.*

instructions

Cutting

From black fabric:
Cut 1 — 13–1/2" x 24–1/2" background rectangle.

From light blue fat quarter:
Cut 1 — 11" x 17" rectangle.

From dark green fabric:
Cut 3 strips — 2–1/2" x 44",
   from the strips cut 2 — 2–1/2" x 24–1/2" border strips
   and 2 — 2–1/2" x 17–1/2" border strips.
Cut 3 strips — 3" x 44" for binding.

From brown fabric:
Cut 16 tongues using template on page 43.

From backing fabric:
Cut 1 — 35" x 24" rectangle.

From paper-backed fusible web:
Cut 1 — 11" x 17" rectangle.

Assembling the Table Runner

1. Sew the 2–1/2" x 24–1/2"
    dark green border strips to the
    top and bottom edges of the
    13–1/2" x 24–1/2" black
    background rectangle as
    shown. Press the seam
    allowances toward the border.

2. Sew 2–1/2" x 17–1/2"
    dark green border strips
    to the left and right edges
    of the background as
    shown. Press the seam
    allowances toward the
    border.

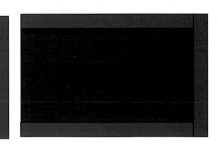

3. Fuse the web rectangle onto the wrong side of the 11" x 17" light blue rectangle, following the manufacturer's instructions. Let cool and fold in half.

4. Place the oval template on page 42 on the folded fabric as indicated. Cut through all layers of the fabric on the curved line; do not cut on the folds.

5. Remove the paper backing from the web. Center and fuse the light blue oval on the right side of the table runner.

Adding the Appliqués

1. Using the appliqué templates on pages 41, 43, and 44, trace the shapes onto the paper side of the fusible web and cut out as directed.

2. Referring to Basic Appliqué instructions on pages 10 and 11, prepare the fabric appliqué pieces. Referring to the photo, position the pieces on the table runner front, fuse in place. Machine appliqué all the fused pieces, including the light blue oval, with matching thread and stabilizer.

3. Position a light brown circle on 8 dark brown tongue pieces as shown; fuse in place. Blanket-stitch by hand or machine around the circles with black thread.

Finishing the Table Runner

1. Layer the backing fabric, batting and appliquéd top. Baste the layers together. Hand- or machine-quilt as desired.

2. With right sides facing, position an appliquéd tongue piece on each of the 8 remaining plain tongue pieces. Sew together the tongue pieces with a 1/4" seam allowance, leaving the straight

edge open. Clip the curves, turn the tongues right side out, and press. Blanket-stitch along the curved edges of each tongue by hand with black perle cotton.

3. Place tongues, appliquéd sides down, on table runner front 1/4" in from each corner as shown. Pin and machine-baste the tongues in place.

4. Sew binding to the edges, following the steps in Basic Binding on page 12 and catching the tongues in the stitching. Tongues will extend beyond the edges of the border as shown when binding is sewn to the back of the table runner.

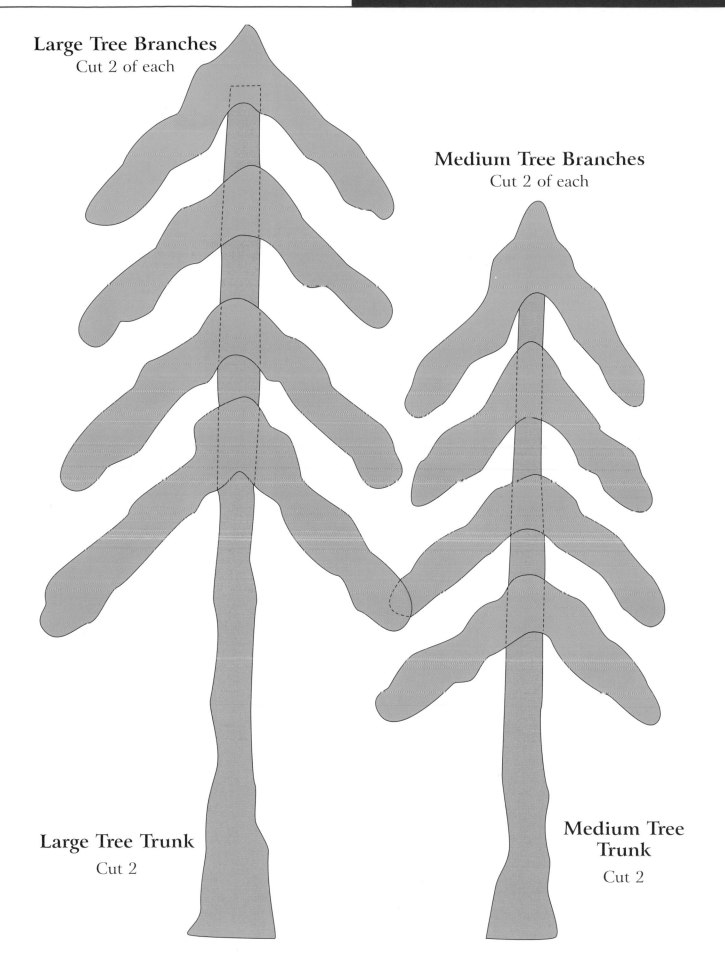

Large Tree Branches
Cut 2 of each

Medium Tree Branches
Cut 2 of each

Large Tree Trunk
Cut 2

Medium Tree Trunk
Cut 2

41

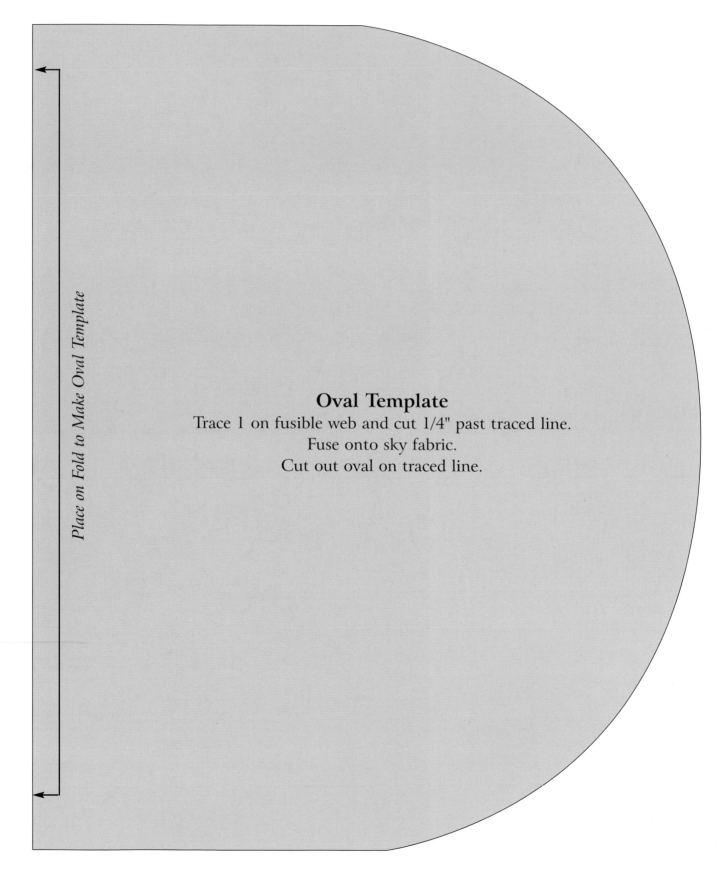

Place on Fold to Make Oval Template

Oval Template
Trace 1 on fusible web and cut 1/4" past traced line.
Fuse onto sky fabric.
Cut out oval on traced line.

Cloud
Cut 1 blue

Ground
Cut 2 brown

Island
Cut 1

Loon Neck &
Chest
Cut 2

Loon
Cut 2

Island
Cut 1

Rock
Cut 1

Rock
Cut 2

Small Tree Branches
Cut 2 of each

Circle for
Tongues
Cut 8

Tongue
Cut 16

Small Tree
Trunk
Cut 2

43

Water
Connect Part A to Part B matching the circles
and dashed lines.
Trace onto fusible web.

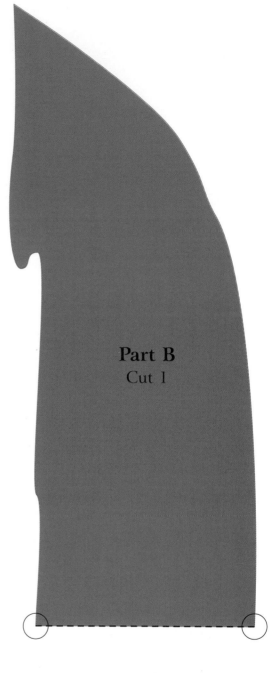

Part B
Cut 1

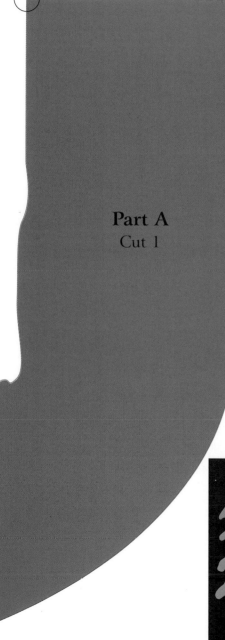

Part A
Cut 1

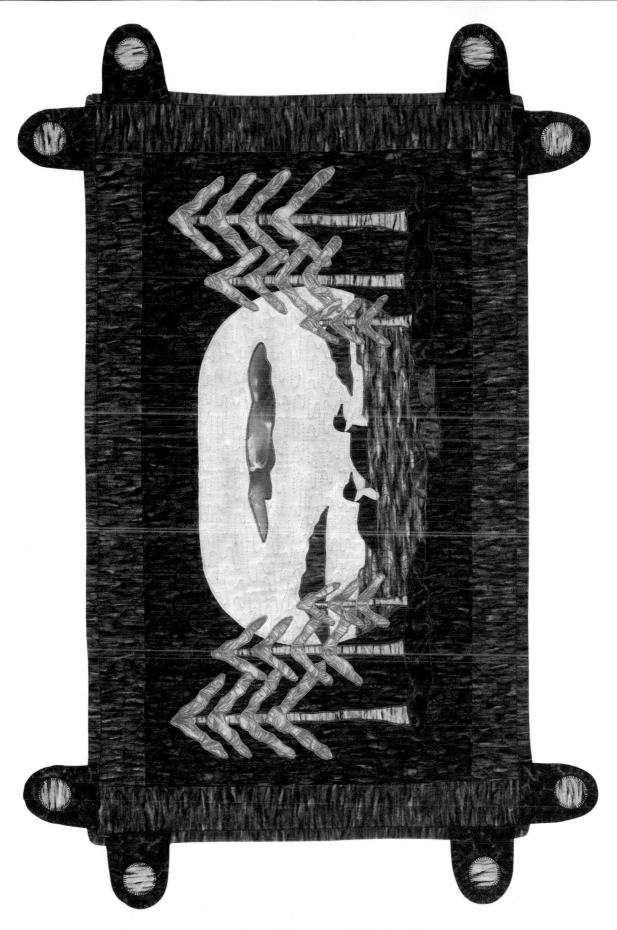

Loons on the Shore Table Runner

table runner
cabin on the lake

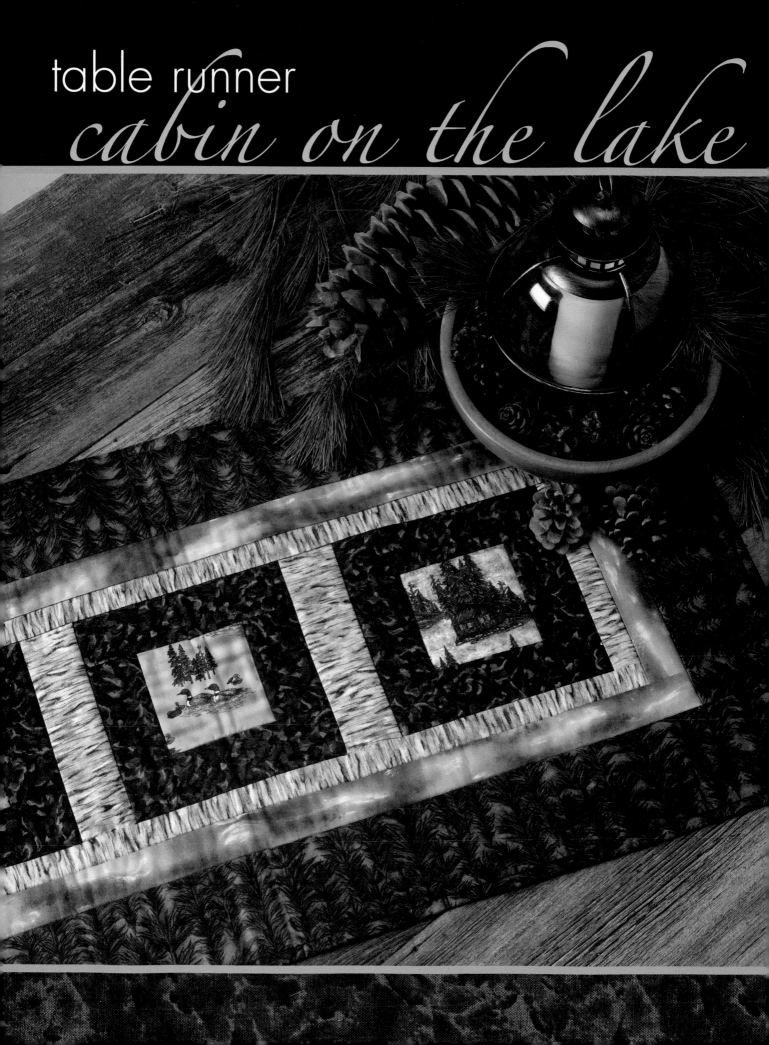

Materials

Finished size is approximately
20-1/2" x 40-1/2"

*Refer to the general instructions on
pages 6–7 before starting this project.*

1/4 yard of lake-motif fabric
for block centers

1/4 yard of dark blue fabric
for blocks

1/4 yard of tan tree bark-motif fabric
for sashing and inner border

1/4 yard of blue fabric
for center border

3/4 yard of dark green fabric
for outer border and binding

1-1/3 yards of backing fabric

27" x 47" piece of batting

*Note: Fabrics are based on 44"-wide
fabrics that have not been washed.
Please purchase accordingly.*

instructions

Cutting

From lake-motif fabric:
Fussy cut 3 — 4-1/2" squares.

From dark blue fabric:
Cut 2 strips — 2-1/2" x 44",
from the strips cut 6 — 2-1/2" x 4-1/2" rectangles
and 6 — 2-1/2" x 8-1/2" rectangles.

From tan fabric:
Cut 1 strip — 2-1/2" x 44" for sashing.
Cut 2 strips — 1-1/2" x 44" for inner border.

From blue fabric:
Cut 3 strips — 2" x 44" for center border.

From dark green fabric:
Cut 3 strips — 4" x 44" for outer border.
Cut 3 strips — 2 1/2" x 44" for binding.

From backing fabric:
Cut 1 — 27" x 47" rectangle.

Assembling the Table Runner Top

1. Sew a 2-1/2" x 4-1/2" dark blue rectangle to the left and right edges of the 4-1/2" lake-motif square as shown. Press the seam allowances toward the rectangles. Repeat to make 3 Unit A.

Make 3 Unit A

2. Sew 2-1/2" x 8-1/2" dark blue rectangles to the top and bottom edges of each Unit A as shown to make 3 Unit B. Press the seam allowances away from the center square.

Make 3 Unit B

3. Sew a 2–1/2"-wide tan sashing strip to the left and right edges of 1 Unit B as shown to make 1 Unit C. Trim to fit and press the seam allowances toward the sashing.

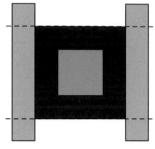

Make 1 Unit C

4. Sew a Unit B to the left and right edges of Unit C as shown. Press the seam allowances toward the sashing strips.

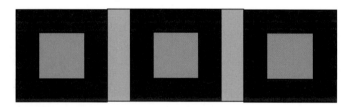

5. Sew a 1–1/2"-wide tan inner border strip to the left and right edges as shown. Trim to fit and press the seam allowances toward the inner border.

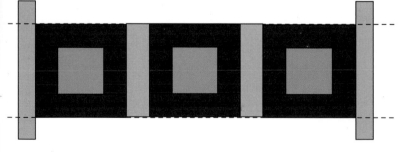

6. Sew a 1–1/2"-wide tan inner border strip to the top and bottom edges as shown. Trim to fit and press the seam allowances toward the inner border.

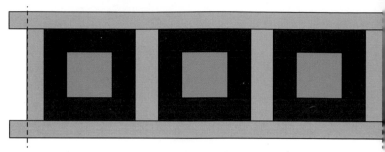

7. Follow Steps 5 and 6 to add the 2"-wide blue center border strips and the 4"-wide dark green outer border strips.

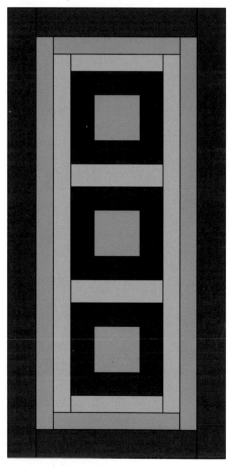

Finishing the Table Runner

Layer the backing fabric, batting and table runner top. Baste the layers together. Hand- or machine-quilt as desired. Finish the table runner by sewing binding to the edges, following the steps in Basic Binding on page 12.

Cabin on the Lake Table Runner

candle mat
sunflower& crow

Materials

Finished size (including tongues)
is approximately
16–1/2" x 19–1/2"

*Refer to the general instructions on
pages 6–/ before starting this project.*

1/3 yard of brown check fabric for
background and backing

3/8 yard of dark brown for tongues

Fabric scraps of
black woodgrain-motif (crow body),
dark brown (wing, flower center),
gold (foot, beak), yellow (flower
petals), and green woodgrain-motif
(stem, leaves)

12" x 15" piece of batting

Lightweight paper-backed
fusible web

Lightweight tear-away stabilizer

Sulky® thread to match appliqués

*Note: Fabrics are based on 44"-wide
fabrics that have not been washed.
Please purchase accordingly.*

instructions

Cutting

From brown check fabric:
   Cut 2 — 11" x 14" rectangles.

From dark brown fabric:
   Cut 36 tongues using the large tongue template on page 117.

Adding the Appliqués

1. Using the appliqué templates on page 52, trace one set of sunflower and crow shapes onto the paper side of the fusible web and cut out as directed.

2. Referring to Basic Appliqué instructions on pages 10 and 11, prepare the fabric appliqué pieces, position them on an 11" x 14" background rectangle, and fuse in place. Machine appliqué with matching thread and stabilizer.

Finishing the Candle Mat

1. With right sides facing, sew the tongue pieces together in pairs with a 1/4" seam allowance, leaving the straight edge open. Clip the curves, turn the tongues right side out, and press. Top-stitch 1/4" from the curved edges of each tongue.

2. Place 4 tongues along each short edge of the candle mat and 5 tongues along each long edge, 1/4" in from the corners as shown. Pin and machine-baste the tongues in place.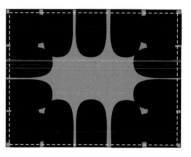

3. Center the backing rectangle right side up on the batting. Place the appliquéd top right side down on the backing. Sew the layers together 1/4" from the fabric edges, leaving the bottom edge open. Trim the batting close to the stitching line and clip the corners. Turn the candle mat right side out, press, and top-stitch the opening closed. Hand- or machine-quilt as desired.

Sunflower and Crow Candle Mat

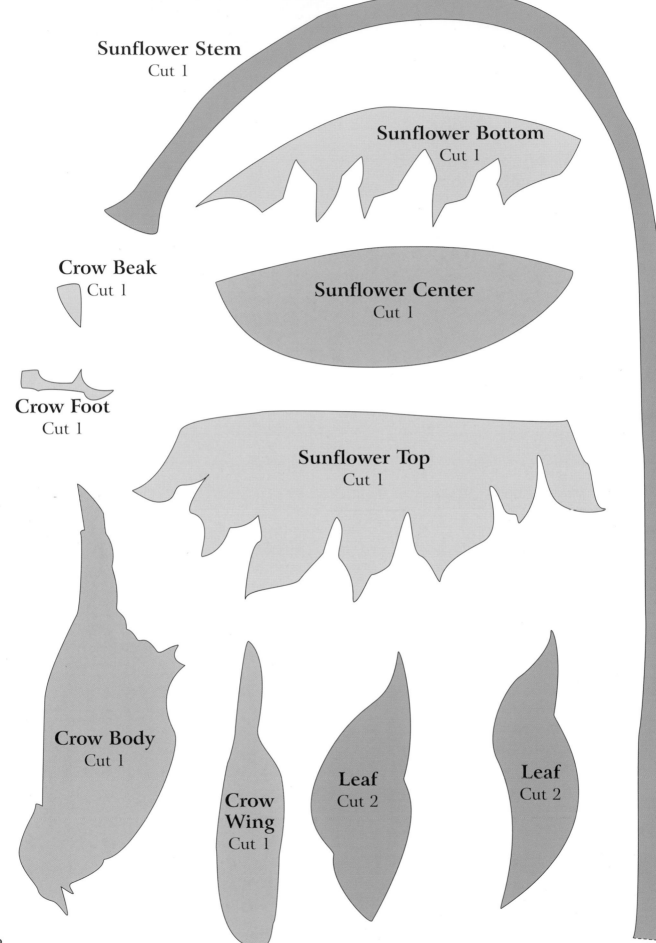

Sunflower Stem
Cut 1

Sunflower Bottom
Cut 1

Crow Beak
Cut 1

Sunflower Center
Cut 1

Crow Foot
Cut 1

Sunflower Top
Cut 1

Crow Body
Cut 1

Crow Wing
Cut 1

Leaf
Cut 2

Leaf
Cut 2

Sunflower & Crow Candle Mat

falling acorns

Materials

Finished size is approximately 47-1/2" x 47-1/2"

Refer to the general instructions on pages 6–7 before starting this project.

1/4 yard each of dark green, tree-motif, and brown woodgrain-motif fabrics for blocks

3/8 yard of tan fabric for background squares

1-1/4 yards of cabin-motif fabric for border

7/8 yard of green fabric for corner triangles and binding

1/8 yard each of rust and orange fabric for leaves

Fabric scraps of green (leaves) and gold and brown (acorns)

3 yards of backing fabric

54" square of batting

Lightweight paper-backed fusible web

Lightweight tear-away stabilizer

Sulky® threads to match appliqués

Note: Fabrics are based on 44"-wide fabrics that have not been washed. Please purchase accordingly.

instructions

Cutting

From dark green fabric:
Cut 2 strips — 3-1/2" x 44",
from the strips cut 17 — 3-1/2" squares.

From each tree-motif and brown woodgrain-motif fabric:
Cut 2 strips — 3-1/2" x 44",
from the strips cut 14 — 3-1/2" squares.

From tan fabric:
Cut 1 strip — 9-1/2" x 44",
from the strip cut 4 — 9-1/2" background squares.

From cabin-motif print:
Cut 4 strips — 10-1/2" x 44",
from the strips cut 4 — 10-1/2" x 27-1/2" border strips.

From green fabric:
Cut 1 strip — 10-7/8" x 44",
from the strip cut 2 — 10-7/8" squares.
Cut squares in half diagonally to make 4 half-square triangles.
Cut 5 strips — 3" x 44" for binding.

From backing fabric:
Cut 2 — 27-1/2" x 54" backing rectangles.

Assembling the Table Topper

1. Arrange 9 — 3-1/2" squares as shown, using three squares of each fabric. Sew the squares together in rows. Press the seam allowances in one direction, alternating the direction from row to row. Sew the rows together to make a Unit A 9-patch block; press. Repeat to make 4 Unit A.

Make 4 Unit A

2. Arrange the remaining 9 — 3-1/2" squares as shown, using 5 dark green, 2 brown woodgrain-motif, and 2 tree-motif. Sew the squares together in rows. Press the seam allowances in one direction, alternating the direction from row to row. Sew the rows together to make 1 Unit B 9-patch block; press.

Make 1 Unit B

3. Sew together 2 Unit A and a 9-1/2" tan background square as shown. Press the seam allowances away from the background square. Repeat to make 2 Unit C.

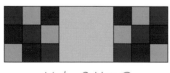

Make 2 Unit C

4. Sew together Unit B and 2 — 9-1/2" tan background squares as shown to make 1 Unit D. Press the seam allowances away from the background squares.

Make 1 Unit D

5. Sew together the 2 Unit C and Unit D as shown to complete the table topper center. Press the seam allowances in one direction.

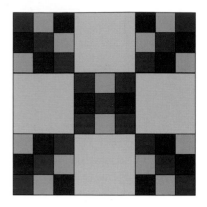

6. Sew a 10-1/2 x 27-1/2" cabin-motif border strip to opposite edges of the table topper center. Take care to attach directional fabric borders with the motifs facing out. Press the seam allowances toward the border.

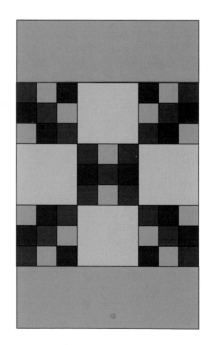

7. Sew a green half-square triangle to each short edge of the two remaining 10-1/2 x 27-1/2" cabin-motif border strips as shown to make 2 Unit E. Press the seam allowances toward the triangles.

Make 2 Unit E

8. Sew a Unit E to the remaining edges of the table topper center. Press the seam allowances toward the border.

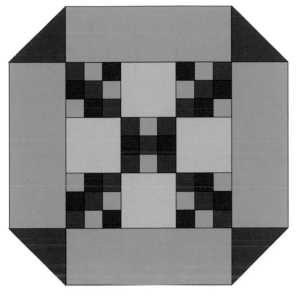

Adding the Appliqués

1. Using the appliqué templates on page 58, trace the shapes onto the paper side of the fusible web and cut out as directed.

2. Referring to Basic Appliqué instructions on pages 10 and 11, prepare the fabric appliqué pieces, position and fuse them on the table topper top, and machine appliqué with matching thread and stabilizer.

Finishing the Table Topper

1. Sew together the 27-1/2" x 54" backing rectangles along one long edge, using a 1/2" seam allowance. Press the seam allowances open.

2. Layer the pieced backing, batting and appliquéd top. Baste the layers together. Hand- or machine-quilt as desired.

3. Sew binding to the edges of the table topper, following the steps in Basic Binding on page 12.

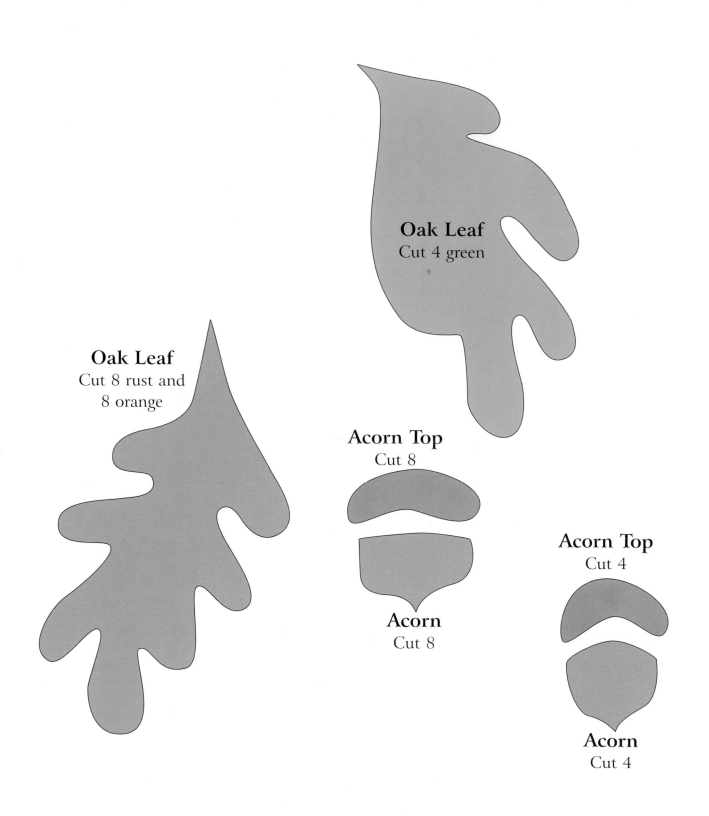

Oak Leaf
Cut 4 green

Oak Leaf
Cut 8 rust and
8 orange

Acorn Top
Cut 8

Acorn
Cut 8

Acorn Top
Cut 4

Acorn
Cut 4

Falling Acorns Table Topper

candle mat
acorns & oak leaves

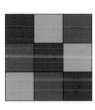

Materials

Finished size is approximately
18–1/2" x 18–1/2"

Refer to the general instructions on pages 6–7 before starting this project.

5/8 yard of brown woodgrain-motif fabric for blocks and binding

1 fat quarter each of green and tree-motif fabrics for blocks

1 fat quarter of tan fabric for background squares

Fabric scraps of rust and green (leaves) and gold and dark brown (acorns)

25" square of backing fabric

25" square of batting

Lightweight paper-backed fusible web

Lightweight tear-away stabilizer

Sulky® threads to match appliqués

Note: Fabrics are based on 44"-wide fabrics that have not been washed. Please purchase accordingly.

instructions

Cutting Instructions

From brown woodgrain-motif fabric:
Cut 1 strip — 3–1/2" x 22"
from strip cut 6 — 3–1/2" squares.
Cut 2 strips — 3" x 44" for binding.

From each green and tree-motif fat quarter:
Cut 1 — 3–1/2" x 22" strip
from strip cut 6 — 3–1/2" squares.

From tan fat quarter:
Cut 2 — 9–1/2" squares.

Assembling the Candle Mat Top

1. Arrange 9 — 3–1/2" squares as shown, using 3 squares of each fabric. Sew the squares together in rows; press the seam allowances in one direction, alternating the direction from row to row. Sew the rows together to make a 9-patch block; press. Repeat to make a second block

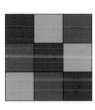

Make 2

2. Sew the 9–1/2" tan squares and the 9-patch blocks together in pairs as shown. Press the seam allowances toward the tan squares.

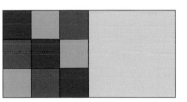

Make 2 Unit A

3. Sew the pairs together to complete the top as shown. Press.

Adding the Appliqués

1. Trace 2 sets of acorns and leaves onto the paper side of the fusible web. Cut out the web shapes about 1/4" beyond the traced lines.

2. Referring to Basic Appliqué instructions on pages 10 and 11, prepare the fabric appliqué pieces, position and fuse the pieces on the candle mat top, and machine appliqué with matching thread.

Finishing the Candle Mat

Layer the backing fabric, batting and appliquéd top. Baste the layers together. Hand- or machine-quilt as desired. Finish the candle mat by sewing binding to the edges, following the steps in Basic Binding on page 12.

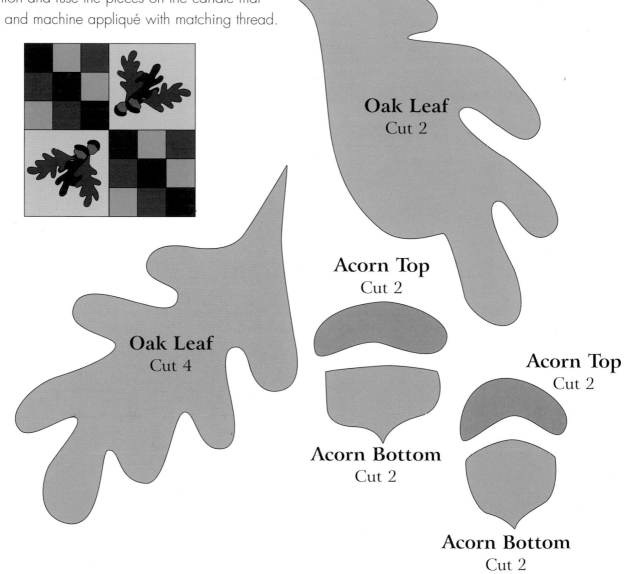

Oak Leaf
Cut 2

Oak Leaf
Cut 4

Acorn Top
Cut 2

Acorn Bottom
Cut 2

Acorn Top
Cut 2

Acorn Bottom
Cut 2

Acorns and Oak Leaves Candle Mat

table topper
pumpkins & bittersweet

Materials

Finished size is approximately
32–1/2" x 32–1/2"

Refer to the general instructions on pages 6–7 before starting this project.

3/8 yard of light yellow fabric
for center

3/8 yard of tan fabric
for center corners

1/4 yard gold fabric
for inner border

7/8 yard of tree-motif fabric
for outer border and binding

14" x 20" piece of dark brown
woodgrain-motif fabric for bittersweet

7" x 22" piece each of rust fabric for
pumpkins and green fabric for leaves

Fabric scraps of dark brown
(pumpkin stems), gold (bittersweet
buds) and orange (centers)

39" square each of backing fabric
and batting

Lightweight paper-backed
fusible web

Lightweight tear-away stabilizer

Sulky thread to match appliqués

*Note: Fabrics are based on
44"-wide fabrics that have not been
washed. Please purchase accordingly.*

instructions

Cutting

From light yellow fabric:
Cut 1 strip — 8–1/2" x 44",
from the strip cut 1 — 8–1/2" x 24–1/2" center rectangle
and 2 — 8–1/2" center squares.

From tan fabric:
Cut 1 strip — 8–1/2" x 44",
from the strip cut 4 — 8–1/2" center corner squares.

From gold fabric:
Cut 4 strips — 1–1/2" x 44",
from the strips cut 2 — 1–1/2" x 24–1/2" inner border strips
and 2 — 1–1/2" x 26–1/2" inner border strips.

From tree-motif fabric:
Cut 4 strips — 3–1/2" x 44",
from the strips cut 2 — 3–1/2" x 26–1/2" outer border strips
and 2 — 3–1/2" x 32–1/2" outer border strips.
Cut 4 strips — 2–3/4" x 44" for binding.

Assembling the Table Topper Top

1. Sew together 2 — 8–1/2" tan corner squares and
   1 — 8–1/2" light yellow center squares as shown. Press
   the seam allowances toward the corner squares. Repeat to
   make a second row of 3 squares.

Make 2

2. Sew the rows from Step 1 to the long edges of the
   8–1/2" x 24–1/2" light yellow center rectangle to
   complete the table topper center as shown. Press the
   seam allowances away from the center rectangle.

3. Sew the 1–1/2" x 24–1/2" gold inner border strips to opposite edges of the table topper center as shown. Press the seam allowances toward the border.

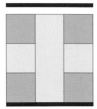

4. Sew the 1–1/2" x 26–1/2" gold inner border strips to the remaining edges of the table topper as shown. Press the seam allowances toward the border.

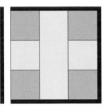

5. Sew the 3–1/2" x 26–1/2" tree-motif outer border strips to opposite edges of the inner border as shown. Press the seam allowances toward the outer border.

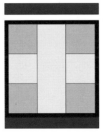

6. Sew the 3–1/2" x 32–1/2" tree-motif outer border strips to the remaining edges of the inner border as shown. Press the seam allowances toward the outer border.

Adding the Appliqués

1. Using the appliqué templates on pages 67, 68, 69, and 70, trace the shapes onto the paper side of the fusible web and cut out as desired.

2. Referring to Basic Appliqué instructions on pages 10 and 11, prepare the fabric appliqué pieces, position and fuse them on the table topper center, and machine appliqué with matching thread and stabilizer.

Finishing the Table Topper

Layer the backing fabric, batting and appliqués top. Baste the layers together. Hand- or machine-quilt as desired. Finish the table topper by sewing binding to the edges, following the steps in Basic Binding on page 12.

**Bittersweet
Layout
Diagram**

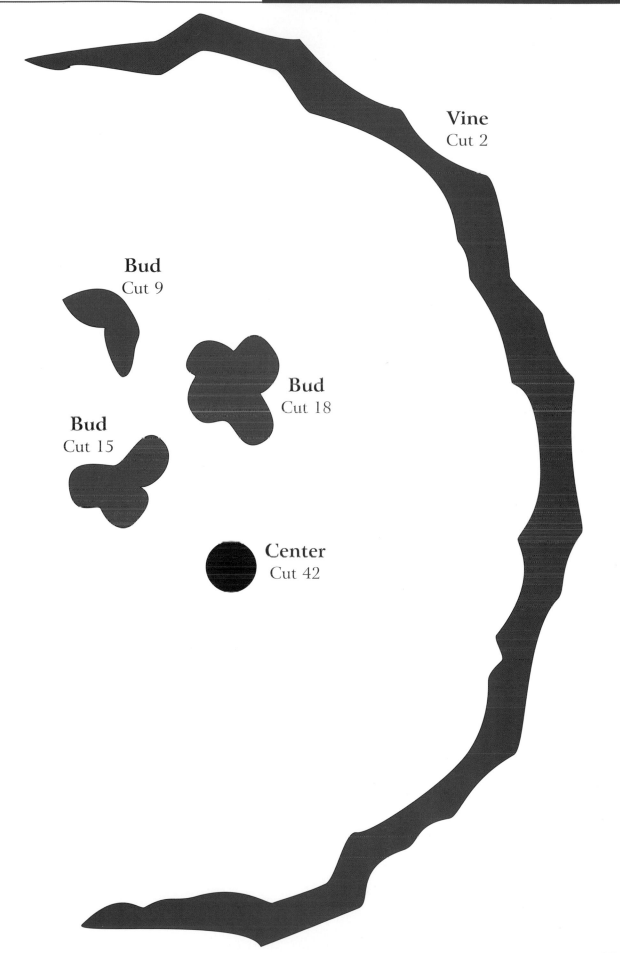

Vine
Cut 2

Bud
Cut 9

Bud
Cut 18

Bud
Cut 15

Center
Cut 42

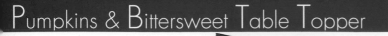

Large Vine
Cut 1 and 1 Reversed

Small Vine
Cut 2

Pumpkin Stem
Cut 4

Pumpkin
Cut 4

Large Leaf
Cut 4

Small Leaf
Cut 4

Pumpkin
Layout
Diagram

Pumpkins & Bittersweet Table Topper

candle mat
bittersweet vines

Materials

Finished size is approximately
16–1/2" x 16–1/2"

*Refer to the general instructions on
pages 6–7 before starting this project.*

3/4 yard yellow fabric
for background, backing and binding

Fat quarter of dark brown
woodgrain-motif fabric for vine

Fabric scraps of gold for bittersweet
buds and orange for centers

21" square of batting

Lightweight paper-backed
fusible web

Lightweight tear-away stabilizer

Sulky® thread to match appliqués

*Note: Fabrics are based on 44"-wide
fabrics that have not been washed.
Please purchase accordingly.*

instructions

Cutting

From light yellow fabric:
    Cut 1 — 16–1/2" background square.
    Cut 1 — 21" backing square.
    Cut 2 strips — 3" x 44" for binding.

Adding the Appliqués

1. Using the appliqué templates for the Pumpkin & Bittersweet Table Topper on pages 75 and 76, trace the shapes onto the paper side of the fusible web and cut out as directed.

2. Referring to Basic Appliqué instructions on pagse 10 and 11, prepare the fabric appliqué pieces, position them on the 16–1/2" light yellow background square, and fuse in place. Machine appliqué with matching thread and stabilizer.

Finishing the Candle Mat

Layer the backing fabric, batting and appliquéd top. Baste the layers together. Hand- or machine-quilt as desired. Finish the candle mat by sewing binding to the edges, following the steps in Basic Binding on page 12.

**Bittersweet
Layout
Diagram**

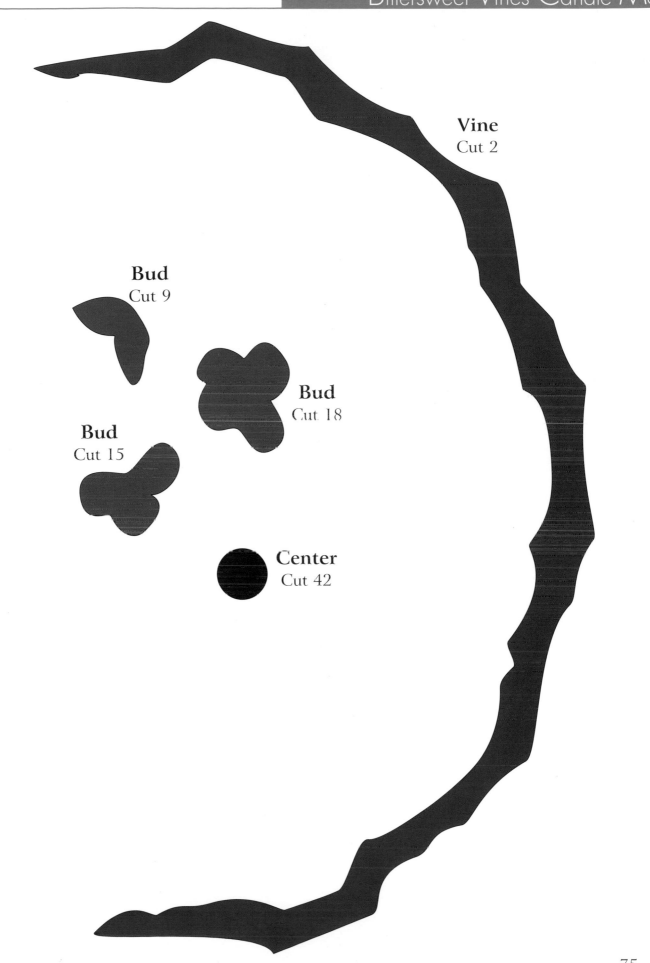

Vine
Cut 2

Bud
Cut 9

Bud
Cut 18

Bud
Cut 15

Center
Cut 42

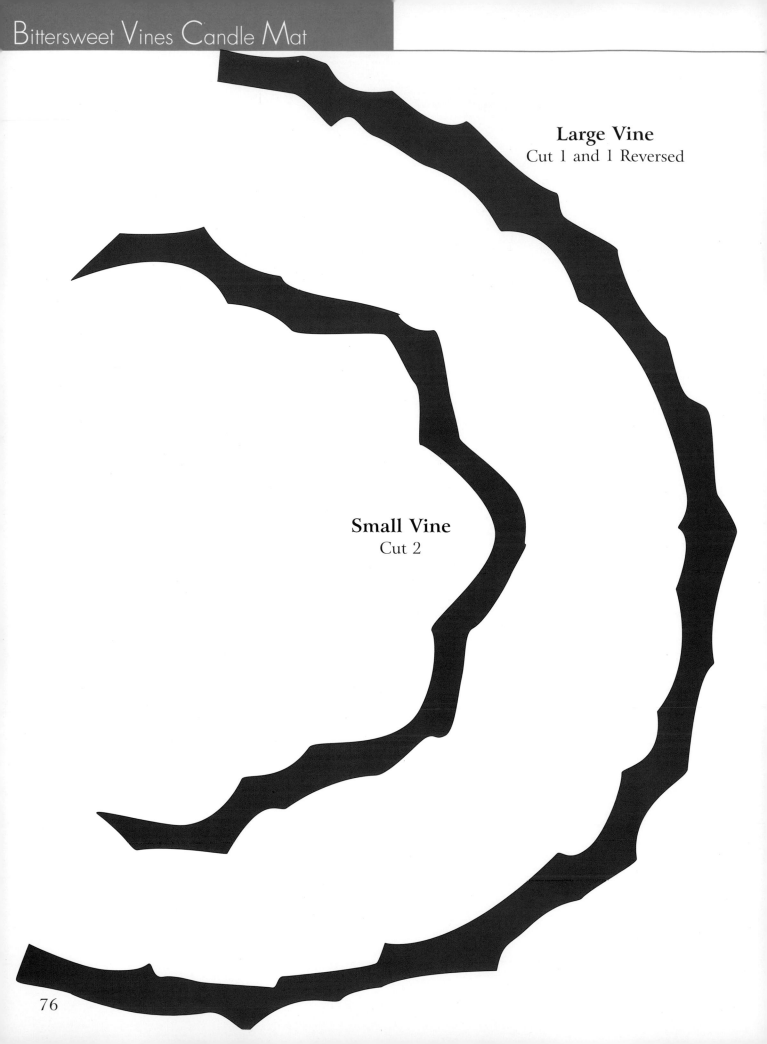

Large Vine
Cut 1 and 1 Reversed

Small Vine
Cut 2

Bittersweet Vines Candle Mat

table runner
autumn beauty

Materials

Finished size is approximately
21" x 48"

Refer to the general instructions on pages 6–7 before starting this project.

1-3/4 yards of dark green fabric
for background and binding

1/2 yard of light yellow fabric
for oval

1/3 yard of green fabric
for long leaf sprigs and branches

1/4 yard of feather-motif fabric
for feathers

Fabric scraps of rust (Chinese Lanterns), dark brown (dried pods), gold (pod centers), and dark green (short leaf sprigs)

1–1/2 yards of backing fabric

27" x 54" piece of batting

2–3/4 yards of 17"-wide
lightweight paper-backed fusible web

Lightweight tear-away stabilizer

Sulky® threads to match appliqués

Note: Fabrics are based on 44"-wide fabrics that have not been washed. Please purchase accordingly.

Cutting

From dark green fabric:
Cut 1 — 21" x 48" rectangle.
Cut 4 strips   2-1/2" x 44" for binding.

From light yellow fabric:
Cut 1 — 15" x 41" rectangle.

From backing fabric:
Cut 1 — 27" x 54" rectangle.

From paper-backed fusible web:
Cut 1 — 15" x 41" rectangle.

Prepare the Table Runner Top

1. Fuse the web rectangle onto the wrong side of the 15" x 41" light yellow rectangle, following the manufacturer's instructions. Let cool and fold in half lengthwise and widthwise.

2. Place the oval template on page 81 on the folded fabric as indicated. Cut through all layers of the fabric on the curved line; do not cut on the folds.

3. Remove the paper backing from the web. Center and fuse the light yellow oval on the right side of the 21" x 48" dark green rectangle.

Adding the Appliqués

1. Using the appliqué templates on pages 82, 83, and 84, trace the shapes onto the paper side of the fusible web and cut out as directed.

2. Referring to Basic Appliqué instructions on pages 10 and 11, prepare the fabric appliqué pieces, position them on the light yellow oval as shown in the diagram, and fuse in place. Machine appliqué all the fused pieces, including the light yellow oval, with matching thread and stabilizer.

Finishing the Table Runner

Layer the backing fabric, batting, and appliquéd top. Baste the layers together. Hand- or machine-quilt as desired. Finish the table runner by sewing binding to the edges following the steps in Basic Binding on page 12.

**Autumn Beauty Table Runner
Layout Diagram**

**Autumn Beauty Table Runner
Oval Template**

Place on Fold to Make Oval Template

Place on Fold to Make Oval Template

Pods & Centers
Cut 1 of each

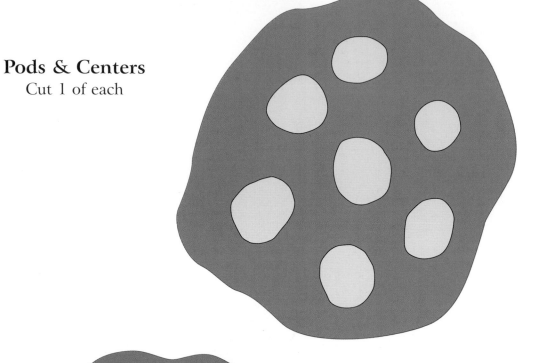

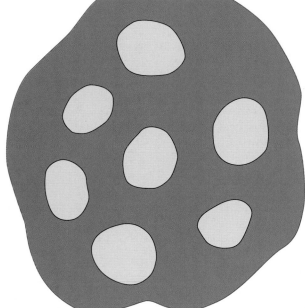

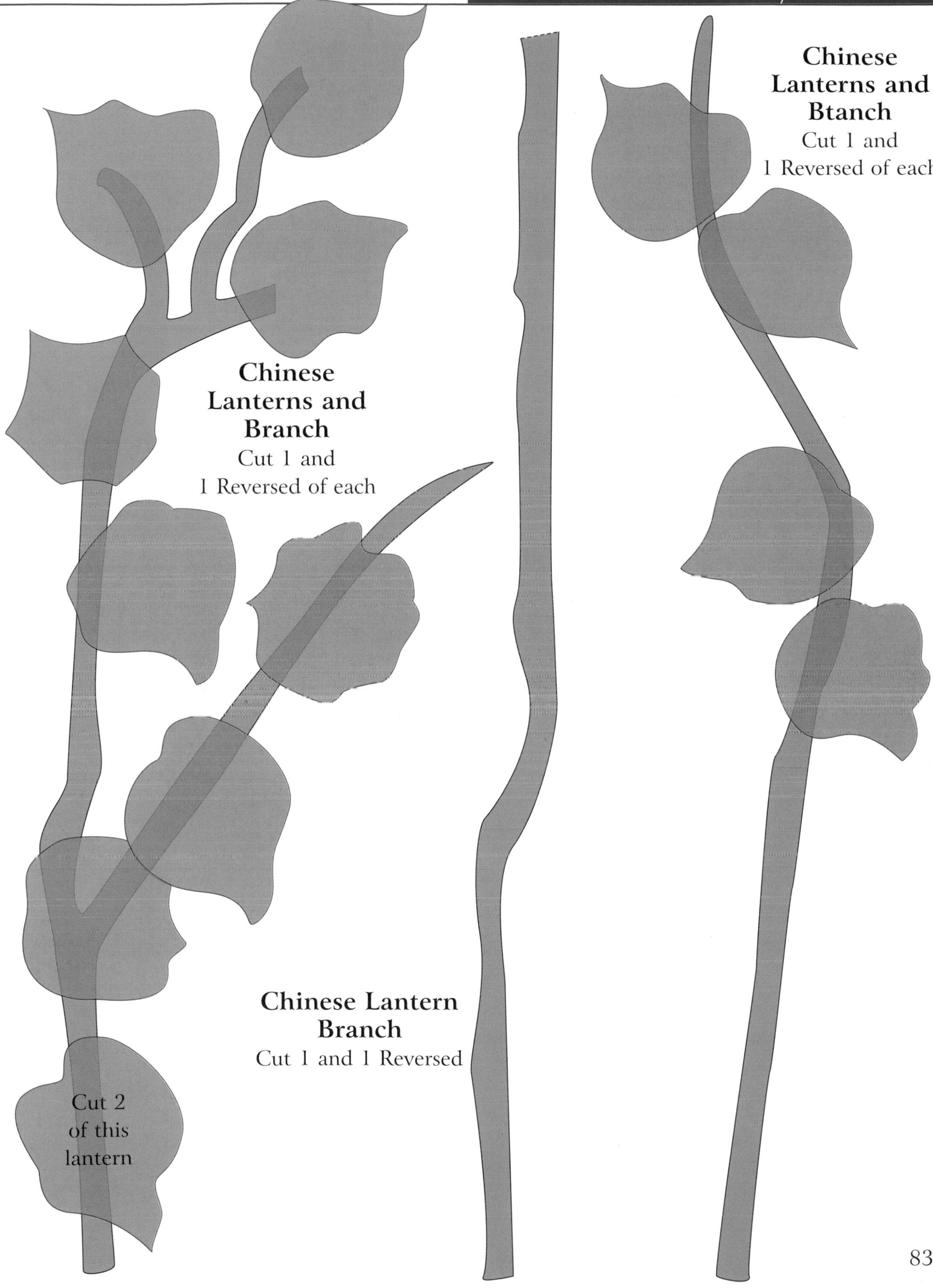

**Chinese
Lanterns and
Btanch**
Cut 1 and
1 Reversed of each

**Chinese
Lanterns and
Branch**
Cut 1 and
1 Reversed of each

**Chinese Lantern
Branch**
Cut 1 and 1 Reversed

Cut 2
of this
lantern

83

Materials

Finished size approximately
26–1/2" x 47–1/2"

*Refer to the general instructions on pages 6–7
before starting this project.*

3/4 yard of orange fabric for
inner pieced border, outer border, and binding

1/8 yard each of green, brown, and gold fabrics
for inner pieced border

3/8 yard of brown check fabric for background

1–1/4 yards of directional tree-motif fabric
for center border

10" square of dark brown woodgrain-motif
fabric for turkey and crow bodies

9"x 11" piece of brown woodgrain-motif
fabric for turkey wings and tail

8" x 18" piece of green for stems and leaves

Fabric scraps of light brown woodgrain-motif (turkey
wings), gold (feet, beaks), red (turkey head),
dark brown (flower center, crow wings),
and yellow (flower petals)

1–1/2 yards of backing fabric

33" x 54" piece of batting

Lightweight paper-backed fusible web

Lightweight tear-away stabilizer

Sulky® threads to match appliqués

*Note: Fabrics are based on 44"-wide fabrics that have
not been washed. Please purchase accordingly.*

Cutting

From orange fabric:
  Cut 5 strips — 2" x 44",
    from strips cut 6 — 2" x 4–1/2" inner border
    rectangles and 2 — 2" x 23–1/2" outer
    border strips.
    Set aside remaining strips.
  Cut 4 strips — 3" x 44" for binding.

From each green, brown, and gold fabric:
  Cut 1 strip — 2" x 44",
    from each strip cut 6 — 2" x 4–1/2" inner
    border rectangles.

From brown check fabric:
  Cut 1 — 12–1/2" x 33–1/2" background rectangle.

From directional tree-motif fabric:
  Cut 2 — 4–1/2" x 44–1/2" center border strips.
    Cut lengthwise from the fabric.
  Cut 2 — 4–1/2" x 15–1/2" center border strips.
    Cut widthwise from the fabric.

From backing fabric:
  Cut 1 — 33" x 54" rectangle.

Assembling the Table Runner Top

1. Using 2 — 2" x 4–1/2" rectangles each of gold,
    brown, and green, sew together the rectangles in
    sets of three as shown to make 2 Unit A. Press the
    seam allowances in one direction.

Make 2 Unit A

2. Sew together the remaining 2" x 4–1/2"
    rectangles as shown in sets of 9 to make 2 Unit
    B. Press the seam allowances in one direction.

Make 2 Unit B

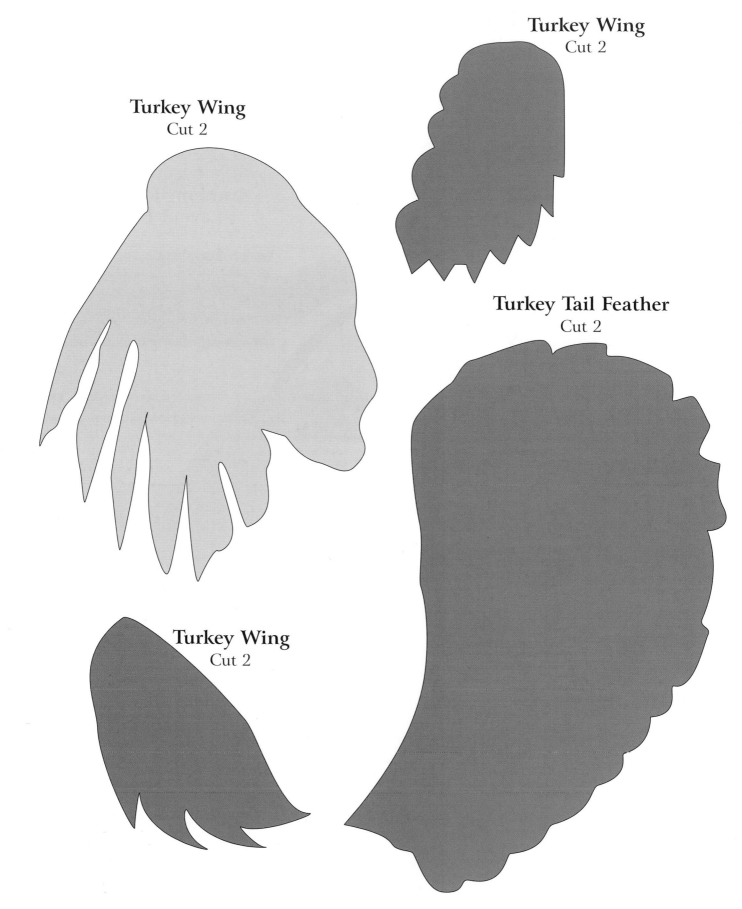

Turkey Wing
Cut 2

Turkey Wing
Cut 2

Turkey Tail Feather
Cut 2

Turkey Wing
Cut 2

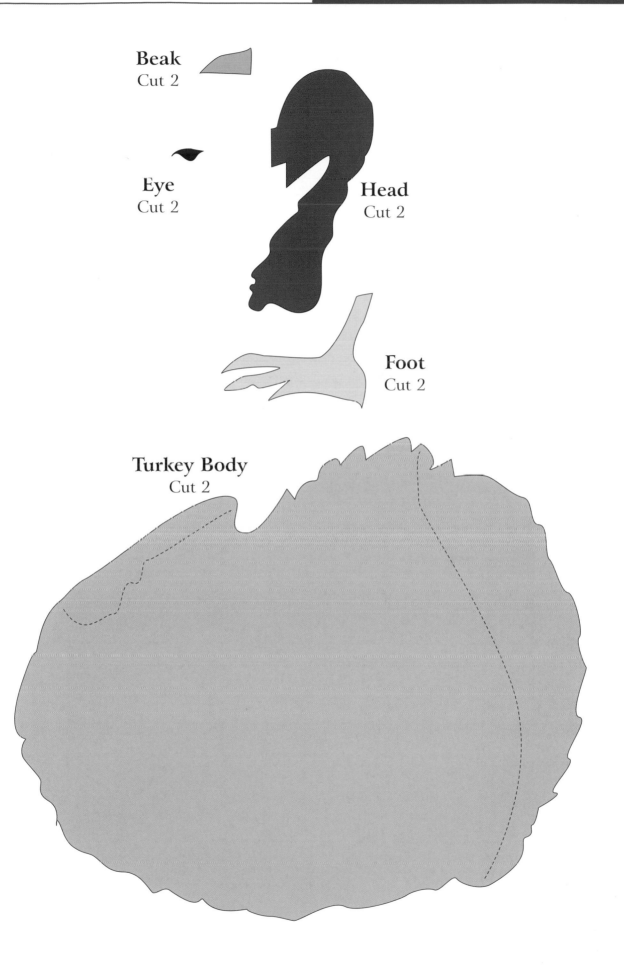

Beak
Cut 2

Eye
Cut 2

Head
Cut 2

Foot
Cut 2

Turkey Body
Cut 2

table runner
stopping to rest

Materials

Finished size is approximately
20–1/2" x 42–1/2"

*Refer to the general instructions on
pages 6–7 before starting this project.*

1/2 yard of cream fabric for center

1/6 yard of dark brown
woodgrain-motif fabric
for inner border

5/8 yard of leaf-motif fabric for outer
border and binding

Fabric scraps of white (bird neck),
black woodgrain-motif (bird wing),
gray (bird body), dark green
woodgrain-motif (sprigs), gold
(pinecones), and black (bird head)

1–1/2 yards of backing fabric

27" x 51" piece of batting

Lightweight paper-backed
fusible web

Lightweight tear-away stabilizer

Sulky® thread to match appliqués

*Note: Fabrics are based on 44"-wide
fabrics that have not been washed.
Please purchase accordingly.*

instructions

Cutting

From cream fabric:
    Cut 1 — 14–1/2" x 36–1/2" background rectangle.

From dark brown woodgrain-motif fabric:
    Cut 3 strips — 1–1/2" x 44",
        from the strips cut 2 — 1–1/2" x 36–1/2" inner border strips
        and 2 — 1–1/2" x 16–1/2" inner border strips.

From leaf-motif fabric:
    Cut 3 strips — 2–1/2" x 44",
        from the strips cut 2 – 2–1/2" x 38–1/2" outer border strips
        and 2 — 2–1/2" x 20–1/2" outer border strips.
    Cut 4 strips — 3" x 44" for binding.

From backing fabric:
    Cut 1 — 27" x 51" rectangle.

Assembling the Table Runner Top

1. Sew the 1–1/2" x 36–1/2" dark brown woodgrain-motif
   inner border strips to the long edges of the 14–1/2" x
   36–1/2" cream background rectangle as shown. Press the
   seam allowances toward the border.

2. Sew the 1–1/2" x 16–1/2" dark brown woodgrain-motif
   inner border strips to the short edges of the background
   rectangle as shown. Press the seam allowances toward
   the border.

3. Sew the 2–1/2" x 38–1/2" leaf-motif outer border strips to the long edges of the inner border. Press the seam allowances toward the outer border.

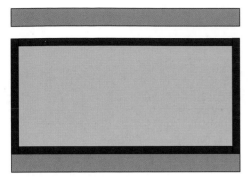

4. Sew the 2–1/2" x 20–1/2" leaf-motif outer border strips to the short edges of the inner border. Press the seam allowances toward the outer border.

Adding the Appliqués

1. Using the appliqué templates on pages 97 and 98, trace the shapes onto the paper side of the fusible web and cut out as directed.

2. Referring to Basic Appliqué instructions on pages 10 and 11, prepare the fabric appliqué pieces, position and fuse them on the cream background rectangle, and machine appliqué with matching thread and stabilizer.

Finishing the Table Runner

Layer the backing fabric, batting and appliquéd top. Baste the layers together. Hand- or machine-quilt as desired. Finish the table runner by sewing binding to the edges, following the steps in Basic Binding on page 12.

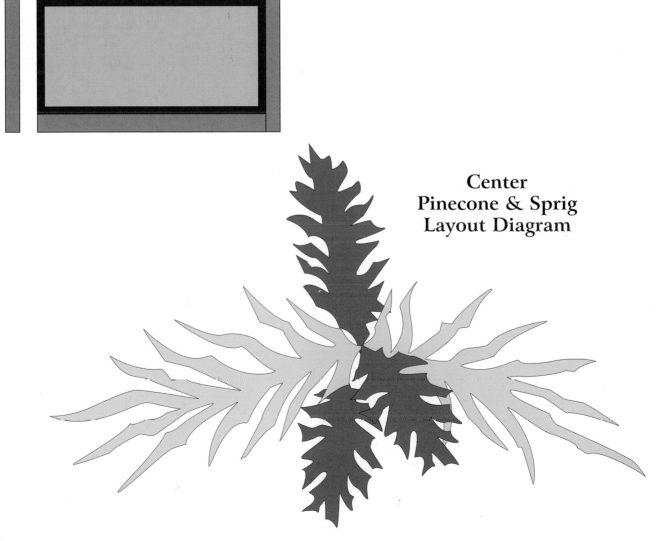

**Center
Pinecone & Sprig
Layout Diagram**

Pine Sprig
Cut 3

Pinc Sprig
Cut 3

Short Pinecone
Cut 2

Tall Pinecone
Cut 3

97

table runner

up north

Materials

Finished size is approximately
18–1/2" x 48–1/2"

*Refer to the general instructions on
pages 6–7 before starting this project.*

1–1/8 yards of tree-motif fabric for
center, outer border, and binding

1/4 yard of blue fabric
for inner border

1 fat quarter of dark green
woodgrain-motif for trees

Fabric scraps of black (bear),
gold (deer), dark brown (moose),
gold (antlers), brown woodgrain-motif
(cabin), tan woodgrain-motif, (door),
light yellow (windows),
brown (tree trunks), and
blue woodgrain-motif (water)

1–1/2 yards of backing fabric

25" x 55" piece of batting

Lightweight fusible web

Lightweight tear-away stabilizer

Sulky® thread to match appliqués

*Note: Fabrics are based on 44"-wide
fabrics that have not been washed.
Please purchase accordingly.*

instructions

Cutting

From tree-motif fabric:
    Cut 1 — 10–1/2" x 40–1/2" center rectangle.
    Cut 3 strips — 3–1/2" x 44",
        from the strips cut 2 — 3–1/2" x 42–1/2" outer border strips
        and 2 — 3–1/2" x 18–1/2" outer border strips.
    Cut 4 strips — 3" x 44" for binding.

From blue fabric:
    Cut 3 strips — 1–1/2" x 44",
        from the strips cut 2 — 1–1/2" x 40–1/2" inner border strips
        and 2 strips 1–1/2" x 12–1/2" inner border strips.

From backing fabric:
    Cut 1 — 25" x 54" rectangle.

Assembling the Table Runner

1. Sew the 1–1/2" x 40–1/2" blue inner border strips to
the long edges of the 10–1/2" x 40–1/2" tree-motif center
rectangle as shown. Press the seam allowances toward
the border.

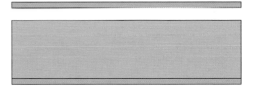

2. Sew the 1–1/2" x 12–1/2" blue inner border strips to the
short edges of the center rectangle as shown. Press the seam
allowances toward the border.

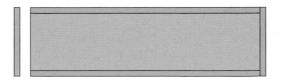

3. Sew the 3–1/2" x 42–1/2" tree-motif outer border strips to the long edges of the inner border. Press the seam allowances toward the outer border.

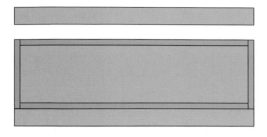

4. Sew the 3–1/2" x 18–1/2" tree-motif outer border strips to the short edges of the inner border. Press the seam allowances toward the outer border.

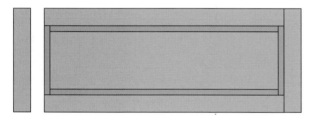

Adding the Appliqués

1. Using the appliqué templates on pages 102, 103, 104, 105 and 106, trace the shapes onto the paper side of the fusible web and cut out as desired.

2. Referring to Basic Appliqué instructions on pages 10 and 11, prepare the fabric appliqué pieces, position and fuse them on the tree-motif center rectangle, and machine appliqué with matching thread and stabilizer.

Finishing the Table Runner

Layer the backing fabric, batting and appliquéd top. Baste the layers together. Hand- or machine-quilt as desired. Finish the table runner by sewing binding to the edges, following the steps in Basic Binding on page 12.

Bear
Cut 1

Moose Body
Cut 1

Moose Antlers
Cut 1

Deer Body
Cut 1

Deer Antlers
Cut 1

Tall Tree
Cut 4

Short Tree
Cut 4

Trunk
Cut 3

Trunk
Cut 4

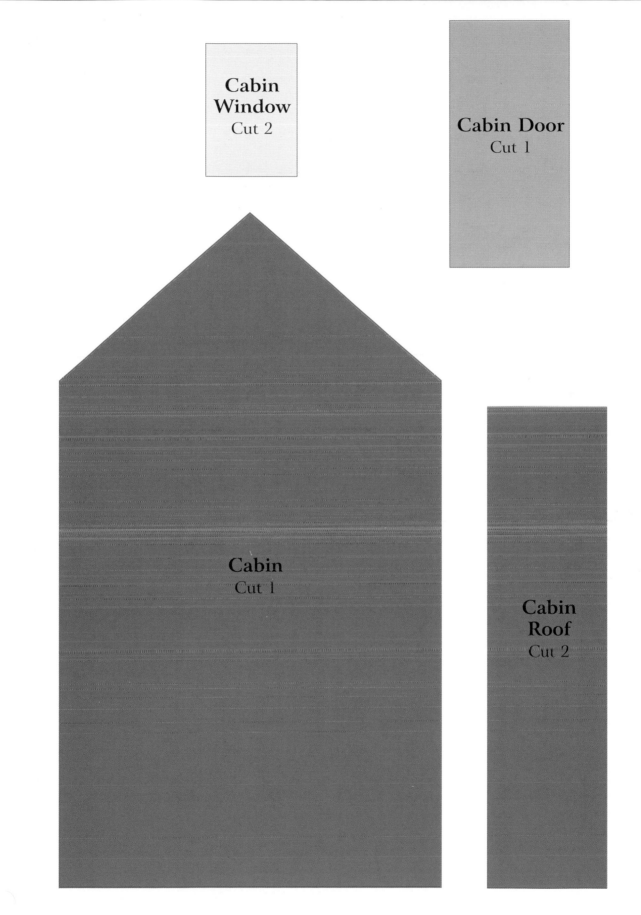

Cabin Window
Cut 2

Cabin Door
Cut 1

Cabin
Cut 1

Cabin Roof
Cut 2

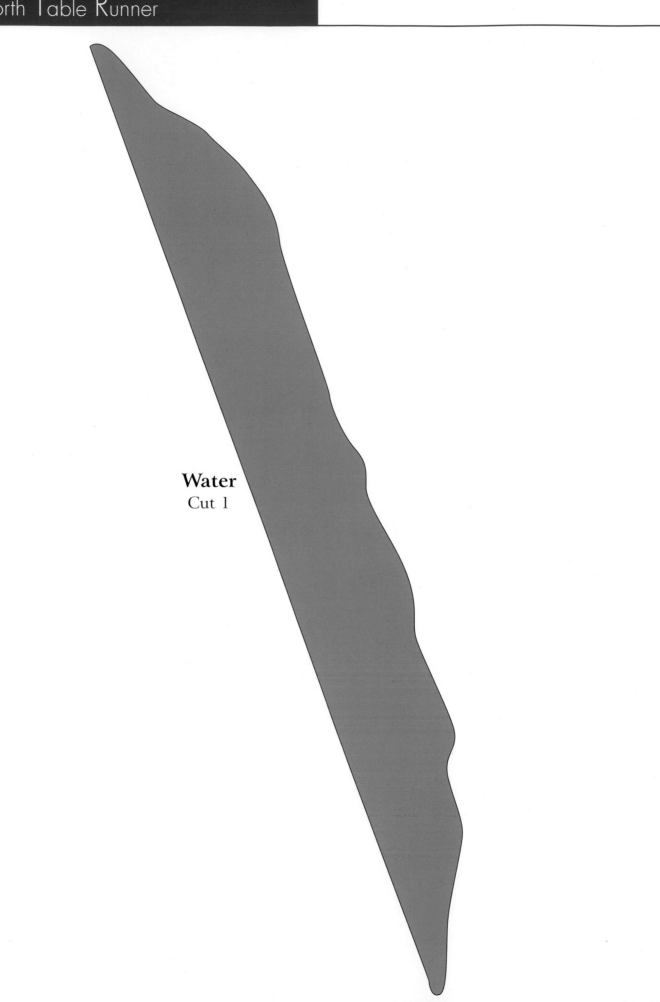

Water
Cut 1

Up North Table Runner

table topper
pine bough

Materials

Finished size is approximately
44-1/2" x 44-1/2"

*Refer to the general instructions on
pages 6–7 before starting this project.*

1 fat quarter each of 1 light blue,
3 medium blues, and
2 dark blues for center

1-1/4 yards of dark green
woodgrain-motif fabric
for border and binding

1 fat quarter each of gold
(pinecones) and light green (sprigs)

3 yards of backing fabric

50" square of batting

Lightweight paper-backed
fusible web

Lightweight tear-away stabilizer

Sulky® thread to match appliqués

*Note: Fabrics are based on 44"-wide
fabrics that have not been washed.
Please purchase accordingly.*

Cutting

From each light, medium, and dark blue fat quarter:
Cut 3 — 4-1/2" x 22" strips,
from the strips cut 11 – 4-1/2" squares.

From dark green woodgrain-motif fabric:
Cut 4 strips — 6-1/2" x 44" for border
and 5 strips — 3" x 44" for binding.

From backing fabric:
Cut 2 — 25-1/2" x 50" backing rectangles.

Assembling the Table Topper Top

1. Sew together 8 — 4-1/2" assorted blue squares to make
one row as shown. Repeat to make 7 additional rows,
scattering the assorted blue squares so each row is different;
there will be 2 extra squares.

Make 8 rows

2. Arrange the rows in a pleasing manner as shown. Press the seam allowances in one direction, alternating the direction from row to row. Sew the rows together to complete the table topper center; press.

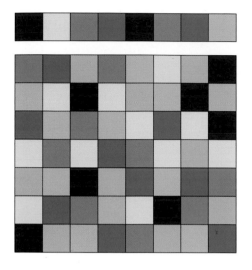

3. Cut 2 — 32–1/2" lengths from the 6–1/2"-wide dark green woodgrain-motif border strips; reserve the extra for Step 4. Sew the 32–1/2" lengths to opposite edges of the table topper center as shown. Press the seam allowances toward the border.

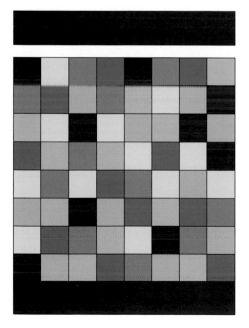

4. Sew together the 2 remaining 6–1/2"-wide dark green wood grain-motif border strips with the reserved pieces from Step 3 to make one long

strip. From the strip, cut 2 — 44–1/2" lengths. Sew these lengths to the remaining edges of the table topper center as shown. Press the seam allowances toward the border.

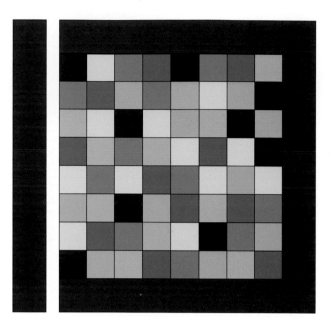

Adding the Appliqués

1. Using the appliqué templates on pages 112, trace the shapes onto the paper side of the fusible web and cut out as directed.

2. Referring to Basic Appliqué instructions on pages 10 and 11, prepare the fabric appliqué pieces, position and fuse them on the table topper top, and machine appliqué with matching thread and stabilizer.

Finishing the Table Topper

1. Sew together the 25-1/2" x 50" backing rectangles along one long edge, using a 1/2" seam allowance. Press the seam allowances open.

2. Layer the pieced backing, batting and appliquéd top. Baste the layers together. Hand- or machine-quilt as desired.

3. Sew binding to the edges of the table topper, following the steps in Basic Binding on page 12.

**Corner
Pinecone & Sprig
Layout Diagram**

**Center
Pinecone & Sprig
Layout Diagram**

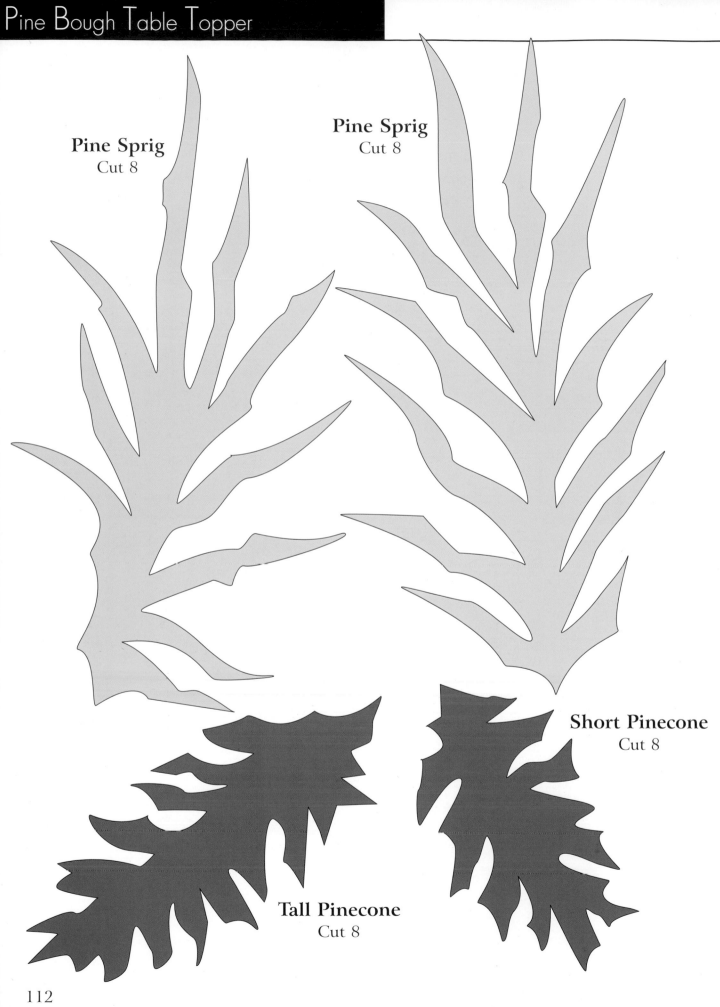

Pine Sprig
Cut 8

Pine Sprig
Cut 8

Short Pinecone
Cut 8

Tall Pinecone
Cut 8

Pine Bough Table Topper

table topper
silent night

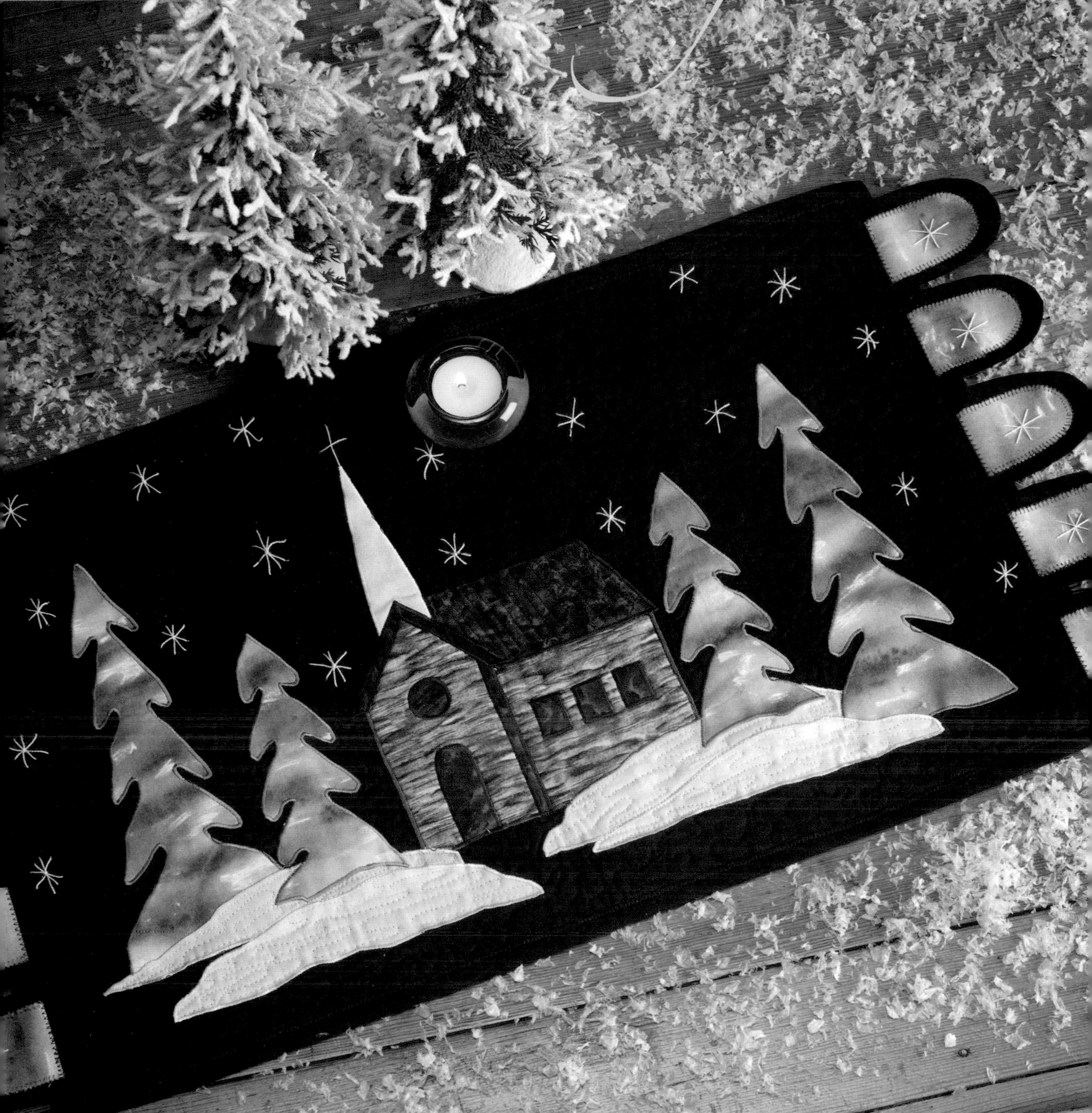

Materials

Finished size is approximately
14–1/2" x 24–1/2"

Refer to the general instructions on pages 6–7 before starting this project.

1–3/8 yards of dark brown fabric for background, tongues, backing and binding

1/4 yard of green fabric for trees and tongues

Fabric scraps of white (snow, steeple), light blue (snow), black (roof trim, circle window), brown (roof, windows, door, corner post), and light brown (church)

20" x 30" piece of batting

Lightweight paper-backed fusible web

Lightweight tear-away stabilizer

Sulky® thread to match appliqués

Off-white DMC Perle Cotton, Size 8

Note: Fabrics are based on 44"-wide fabrics that have not been washed. Please purchase accordingly.

Cutting

From dark brown fabric:
Cut 1 rectangle — 14–1/2" x 24–1/2" for background.
Cut 1 rectangle — 20" x 30" for backing.
Cut 3 strips — 2–3/4" x 44" for binding.
Cut 20 tongues using template on page 117.

Adding the Appliqués

1. Using the appliqué templates on pages 116, 117, and 118, trace the shapes for the table topper front and tongues onto the paper side of the fusible web and cut out as directed.

2. Referring to Basic Appliqué instructions on pages 10 and 11, prepare the fabric appliqué pieces. Referring to the photo and diagram below, position the pieces on the 14–1/2" x 24–1/2" dark brown background rectangle and fuse in place. Machine appliqué all the fused pieces with matching thread.

3. Position a green tongue appliqué on 10 dark brown tongues as shown; fuse in place. Blanket-stitch by hand or machine along the curved edges of the fused green tongues.

4. Hand-embroider snowflakes on appliquéd table topper front and on each green appliquéd tongue with off-white perle cotton.

Finishing the Table Topper

1. Layer the backing rectangle, batting and appliquéd top. Baste the layers together. Hand- or machine-quilt as desired.

2. With right sides facing, position an appliquéd tongue piece on each of the 10 remaining plain tongue pieces. Sew the tongue pieces together with a 1/4" seam allowance, leaving the straight edge open. Clip the curves, turn the tongues right side out and press.

3. Place 5 tongues, appliquéd sides down, along each short edge of the table topper front, 1/4" in from the corners as shown. Pin and machine-baste the tongues in place.

4. Sew binding to the edges, following the steps in Basic Binding on page 12 and catching the tongues in the stitching. Tongues will extend beyond the edges of the border as shown when binding is sewn to the back of the table runner.

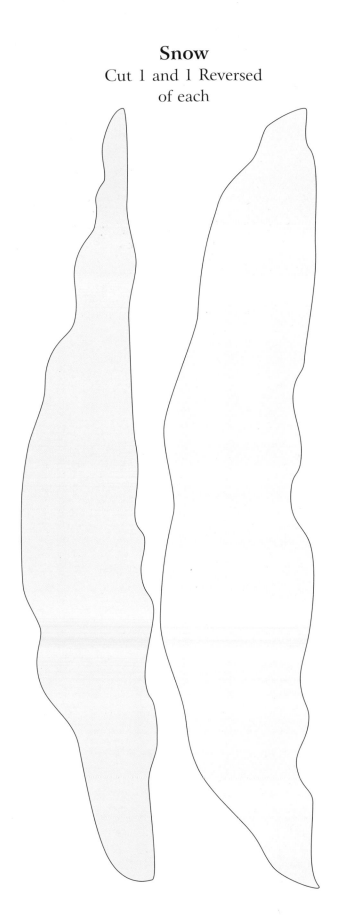

Snow
Cut 1 and 1 Reversed
of each

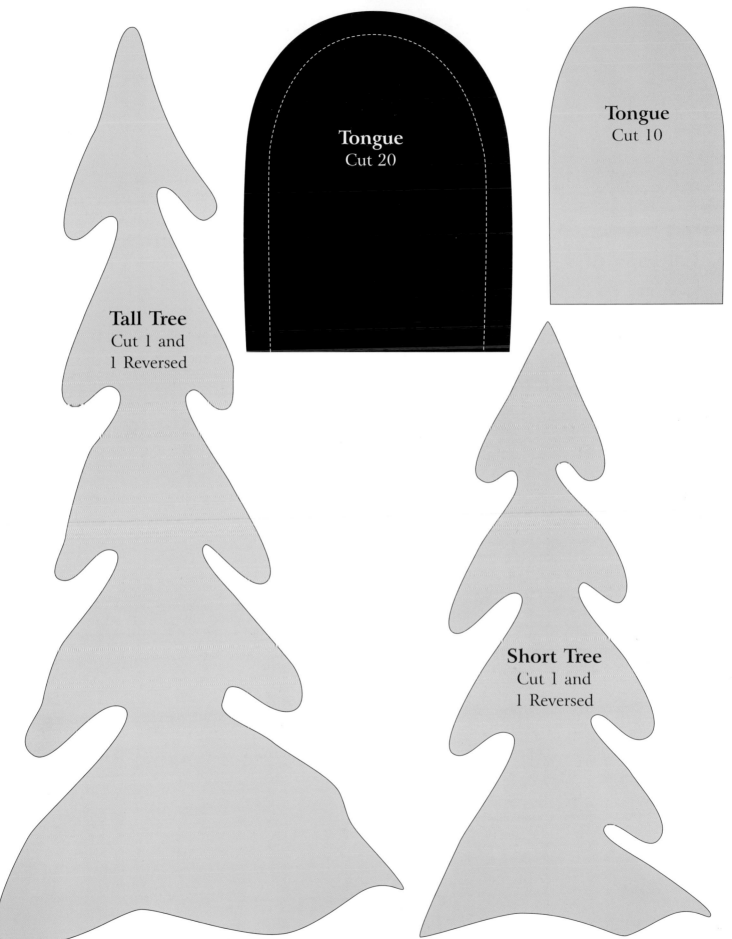

Tongue
Cut 20

Tongue
Cut 10

Tall Tree
Cut 1 and
1 Reversed

Short Tree
Cut 1 and
1 Reversed

117

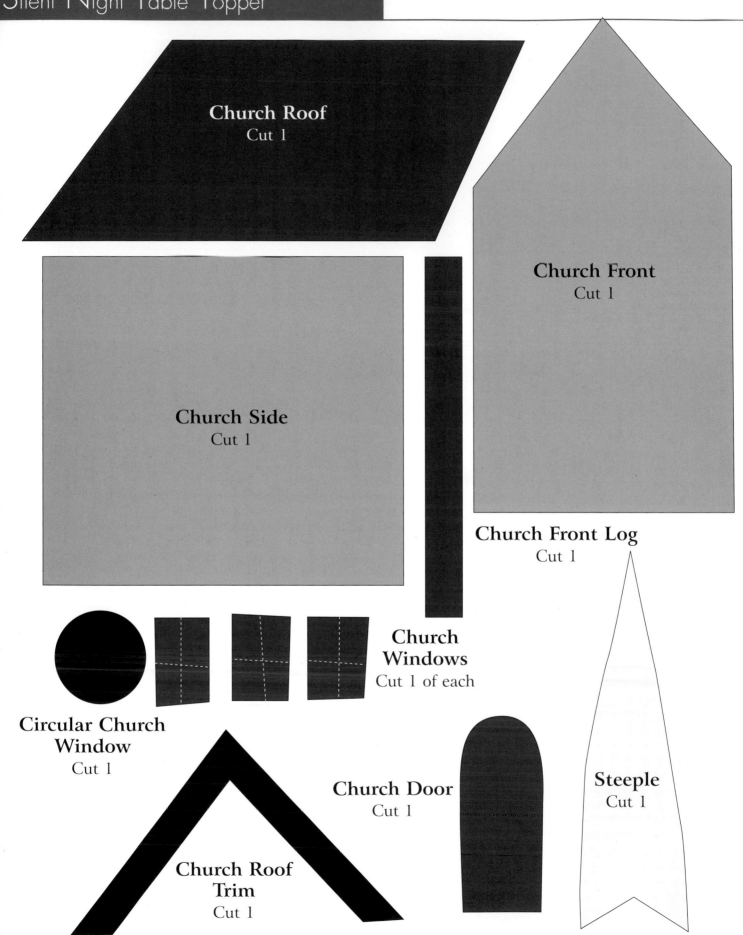

Church Roof
Cut 1

Church Front
Cut 1

Church Side
Cut 1

Church Front Log
Cut 1

Church Windows
Cut 1 of each

Circular Church Window
Cut 1

Church Door
Cut 1

Steeple
Cut 1

Church Roof Trim
Cut 1

Silent Night Table Topper

table runner
winter's here

Materials

Finished size is approximately
18-1/2" x 41-1/2"

Refer to the general instructions on pages 6–7 before starting this project.

5/8 yard of dark blue fabric for block centers and binding

1/8 yard of white fabric for block corners

3/8 yard of blue cloud-motif for sashing and inner border

1 fat quarter each of 5 assorted blue fabrics for outer border

Fabric scraps of white (snowflakes), green, red, and gold (mittens), dark brown (strings), light brown (cuffs), gray (skate cuff, blades), dark brown (soles), and tan (skates)

1-1/3 yards of backing fabric

25" x 48" piece of batting

Lightweight paper-backed fusible web

Lightweight tear-away stabilizer

Sulky® thread to match appliqués

Note: Fabrics are based on 44"-wide fabrics that have not been washed. Please purchase accordingly.

instructions

Cutting

From dark blue fabric:
Cut 1 strip — 9-1/2" x 44",
from the strip cut 3 — 9-1/2" center squares.
Cut 3 strips — 2-1/2" x 44" for binding.

From white fabric:
Cut 1 strip — 3" x 44",
from the strip cut 12 — 3" corner squares.

From blue cloud-motif fabric:
Cut 3 strips — 3" x 44",
from the strips cut 4 — 3" x 9-1/2" sashing and inner border strips and
2 — 3" x 37-1/2" inner border strips.

From each blue fat quarter:
Cut 2 strips — 2-1/2" x 22",
from the strips cut 6 — 2-1/2" x 4-1/2" outer border rectangles.

From backing fabric:
Cut 1 — 25" x 48" rectangle.

Assembling the Table Runner Top

1. Use a pencil to lightly draw a diagonal line on the wrong side of each 3" white corner square as shown.

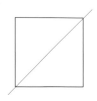

2. With right sides facing, position a white corner square at one corner of a 9–1/2" dark blue center square. Sew on the drawn line as shown.

3. Flip the inside half of the white square to the outside, aligning all edges of the white square with the edges of the dark blue square and creating a white triangle as shown; press. Trim the seam allowance of the middle layer (white square) to 1/4".

4. Repeat Steps 2 and 3 to make a triangle at each corner of each of the 3 — 9–1/2" dark blue center squares to make 3 blocks as shown.

5. Sew together 3 blocks and 4 — 3" x 9–1/2" blue cloud-motif sashing and inner border strips to complete the table runner center as shown. Press the seam allowances toward the blue cloud-motif strips.

6. Sew the 3" x 37–1/2" blue cloud-motif inner border strips to the long edges of the table runner center as shown. Press the seam allowances toward the border.

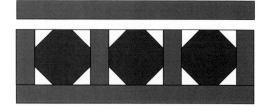

7. Sew the 2–1/2" x 4–1/2" assorted blue outer border rectangles together in a pleasing manner to make one long strip. Press all seam allowances in the same direction.

8. From the pieced outer border strip from Step 7, cut 2 — 37–1/2" lengths. Sew the lengths to the long edges of the inner border as shown. Press the seam allowances toward the inner border.

9. Cut 2 — 18-1/2" lengths from the remaining pieced outer border strip. Sew these lengths to the short edges of the inner border as shown. Press the seam allowances toward the inner border.

Adding the Appliqués

1. Using the appliqué templates on pages 124, 125, and 126, trace the shapes onto the paper side of the fusible web and cut out as desired.

2. Referring to Basic Appliqué instructions on pages 10 and 11, prepare the fabric appliqué pieces, position and fuse them on the table runner top, and machine appliqué with matching thread and stabilizer.

Finishing the Table Runner

Layer the backing fabric, batting and appliquéd top. Baste the layers together. Hand- or machine-quilt as desired. Finish the table runner by sewing binding to the edges, following the steps in Basic Binding on page 12.

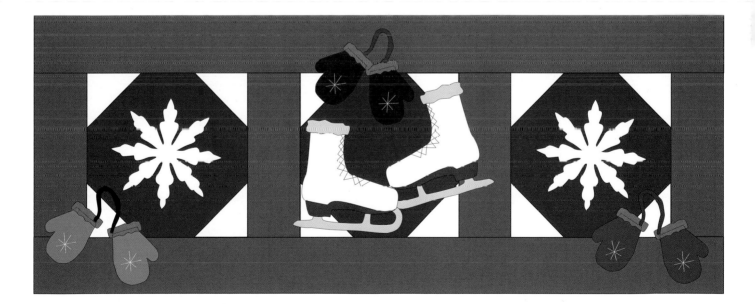

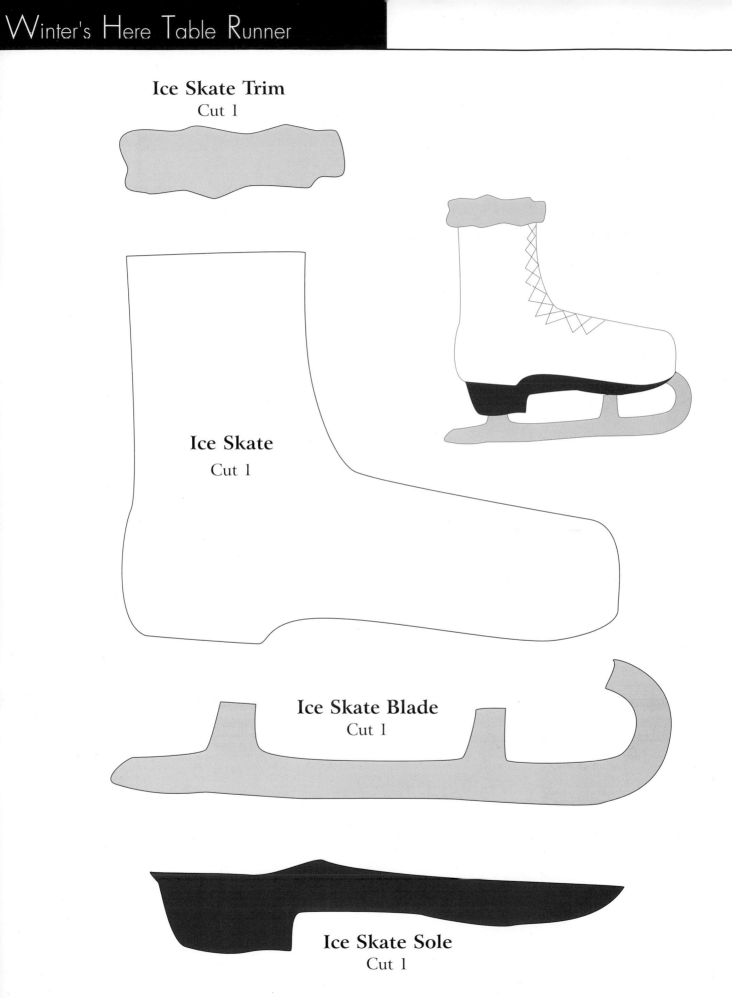

Ice Skate Trim
Cut 1

Ice Skate
Cut 1

Ice Skate Blade
Cut 1

Ice Skate Sole
Cut 1

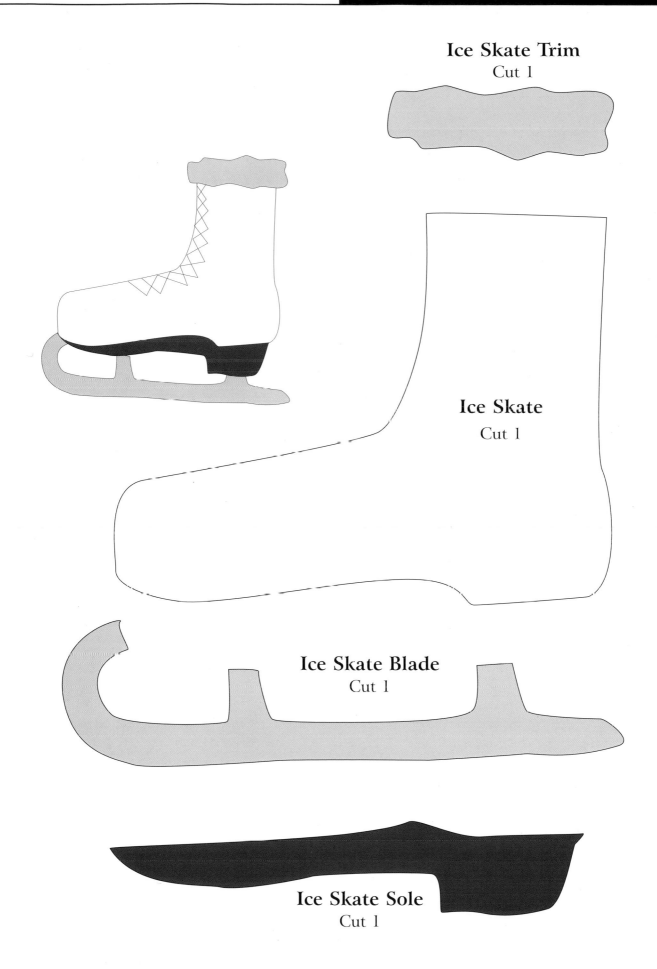

Ice Skate Trim
Cut 1

Ice Skate
Cut 1

Ice Skate Blade
Cut 1

Ice Skate Sole
Cut 1

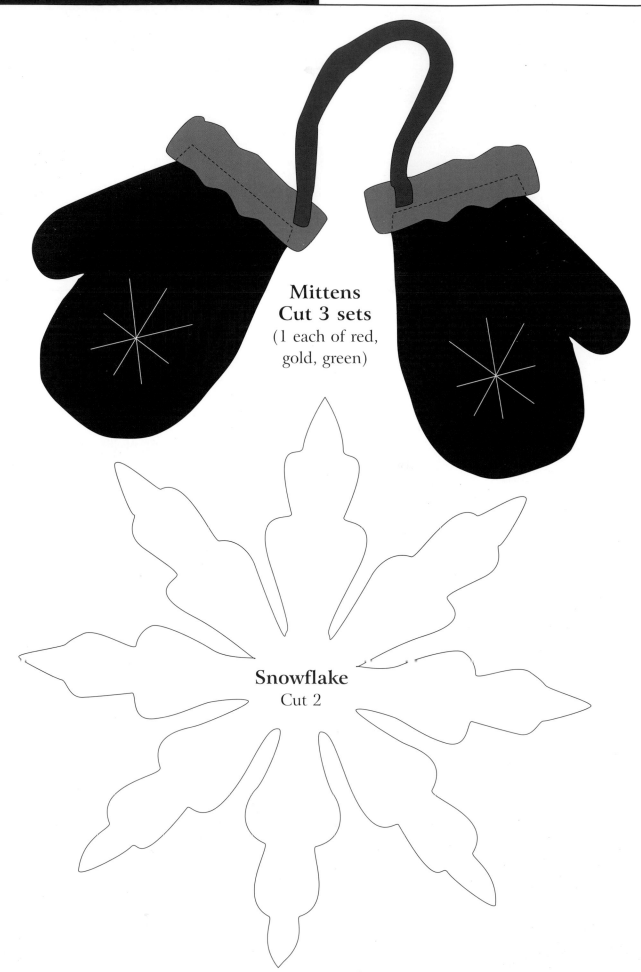

**Mittens
Cut 3 sets**
(1 each of red,
gold, green)

Snowflake
Cut 2